THE RESURRECTION OF THE LORD

The Resurrection of the Lord
Mystery of Faith

Pierre R. Bernard, OP

Translated by
Francis V. Manning, MA, STB

ALBA·HOUSE   NEW·YORK

SOCIETY OF ST. PAUL, 2187 VICTORY BLVD., STATEN ISLAND, NEW YORK 10314

Library of Congress Cataloging-in-Publication Data

Bernard, Pierre R.
  The Resurrection of the Lord: mystery of faith / Pierre R.
Bernard; translated by Francis V. Manning.
      p.   cm.
  Excerpt from the author's The mystery of Jesus first published in
French in 1957.
    ISBN 0-8189-0741-X
    1. Jesus Christ — Resurrection.   I. Bernard, Pierre R. Mystère de
Jésus.   II. Title.
  BT481.B455   1996
  232'.5 — dc20   96-785
                                                      CIP

Produced and designed in the United States of America by the
Fathers and Brothers of the Society of St. Paul,
2187 Victory Boulevard, Staten Island, New York 10314,
as part of their communications apostolate.

ISBN: 0-8189-0741-X

Printing Information:

Current Printing - first digit   1   2   3   4   5   6   7   8   9   10

Year of Current Printing - first year shown

1996   1997   1998   1999   2000   2001

TABLE OF CONTENTS

INTRODUCTION

The Resurrection of the Lord is an excerpt from a much larger work, *The Mystery of Jesus*, about which a few words need to be said.

Pierre Rogatien Bernard (1888-1966) was a French Dominican and author. An earlier work of his, *The Mystery of Mary*, was published in English translation by Herder in 1960. His main work, however, was *The Mystery of Jesus*, which was first published in French in 1957. Alba House published the English language version in 1966, with a second printing in 1967. The work has been out of print for many years now.

The Mystery of Jesus is a massive work in two volumes (507 and 544 pages respectively), with small type set in 51 lines per page. To give an idea of its size, the present work, *The Resurrection of the Lord*, represents pp. 449-514 of volume two.

In his Translator's Preface to *The Mystery of Jesus*, Fr. Francis V. Manning summed up Father Bernard's unique approach to writing about the Savior:

> Has Father Bernard... gone contrary to the tenets of modern exegesis by fashioning a biography of Jesus? At first glance it may seem so. And yet he speaks not so much of a "life" of Jesus as of the "Mystery" of Jesus. While he does present a kind of geographical-chronological framework, and his interpretation accepts the various accounts pretty much at face value, the main emphasis is upon the gradual unfolding of the manifold implications embraced within the Person of Christ....

[His] chief concern is to make the Christ live for us in all his simplicity, grandeur and love... As we read these pages forged in the meditation of Father Bernard upon the text of the Gospel, we may here and there question his interpretation, but we cannot challenge the realness of the divinity and humanity of Jesus which he so successfully discovers to us; we can only joyfully accept it and acknowledge our gratitude to him for carrying us a bit further into the mystery of Jesus.

The following section of *The Mystery of Jesus*, dealing with Christ's Resurrection and Ascension, can stand on its own as a separate work. It can be read and enjoyed without having to go through hundreds of other pages. May *The Resurrection of the Lord* bring Fr. Bernard's prayerful insights to a new generation.

Bro. Frank Sadowski, SSP
Staten Island, NY

Biblical Abbreviations

OLD TESTAMENT

Genesis	Gn	Nehemiah	Ne	Baruch	Ba
Exodus	Ex	Tobit	Tb	Ezekiel	Ezk
Leviticus	Lv	Judith	Jdt	Daniel	Dn
Numbers	Nb	Esther	Est	Hosea	Ho
Deuteronomy	Dt	1 Maccabees	1 M	Joel	Jl
Joshua	Jos	2 Maccabees	2 M	Amos	Am
Judges	Jg	Job	Jb	Obadiah	Ob
Ruth	Rt	Psalms	Ps	Jonah	Jon
1 Samuel	1 S	Proverbs	Pr	Micah	Mi
2 Samuel	2 S	Ecclesiastes	Ec	Nahum	Na
1 Kings	1 K	Song of Songs	Sg	Habakkuk	Hab
2 Kings	2 K	Wisdom	Ws	Zephaniah	Zp
1 Chronicles	1 Ch	Sirach	Si	Haggai	Hg
2 Chronicles	2 Ch	Isaiah	Is	Malachi	Ml
Ezra	Ezr	Jeremiah	Jr	Zechariah	Zc
		Lamentations	Lm		

NEW TESTAMENT

Matthew	Mt	Ephesians	Eph	Hebrews	Heb
Mark	Mk	Philippians	Ph	James	Jm
Luke	Lk	Colossians	Col	1 Peter	1 P
John	Jn	1 Thessalonians	1 Th	2 Peter	2 P
Acts	Ac	2 Thessalonians	2 Th	1 John	1 Jn
Romans	Rm	1 Timothy	1 Tm	2 John	2 Jn
1 Corinthians	1 Cor	2 Timothy	2 Tm	3 John	3 Jn
2 Corinthians	2 Cor	Titus	Tt	Jude	Jude
Galatians	Gal	Philemon	Phm	Revelation	Rv

THE RESURRECTION OF THE LORD

CHAPTER 1

THE MYSTERY OF THE RESURRECTION

The Preaching of the Resurrection

The mystery of Jesus condemned to an ugly death and enclosed in a beautiful tomb is not closed either with this death or with this tomb.

At the time of Pentecost, fifty days after the Pasch, Peter already preached the gospel of the Resurrection. Luke has conserved for us, at the debut of the Acts, the style and the features of this initial annunciation. Filled with the Holy Spirit (Ac 4:8), showing himself at one and the same time a worthy man and a great lord, Peter spoke a direct language, bearing the imprint of a great deal of strength, exempt from all violence; no bitterness, no vituperation, a surprising serenity, a cordial invitation, an admirable lifting of the spirit, a measured view of things, a discourse of wisdom:

> Gentlemen of Judea and all of you who are sojourning in Jerusalem, put yourselves in the spirit of the thing which you behold, listen to what I am going to say... My dear Israelites, hear me well... Jesus the Nazarene, the man whom God has accredited in your midst by the powers, prodigies and signs which he had given him to exercise among you as you yourselves know; this man whom, having been delivered to you according to the plan fixed in the divine foreknowledge, you have brought to death by crucifying him through the hands of pagans, God has raised up in delivering him from the throes of death, be-

cause it was not truly possible that it hold him in its power
(Ac 2:14, 22-24).

Peter then cites certain passages from a Psalm:

You will not leave my soul in Hades, and you will not
allow that your holy one see corruption. (Ps 16:8-11).

He then adds:

Gentlemen, my brothers, it is permissible to say before
you in all liberty, this patriarch David (whom I quote),
well! he died and was interred, even today his monument
still being among you. Only, as he was a prophet and he
knew that God had promised him with an oath to have
someone of his own [David's] race sit upon his [God's]
throne, in advance he saw the resurrection of the Christ
and he spoke of it, giving assurance that this Christ would
not be left in Hades and that his flesh would not know
corruption. This Jesus, God has raised up; of this all of us
are the witnesses (Ac 2:29-32).

Several days later, at the Beautiful Door of the Temple, the
same Peter having healed a helpless man simply by the application of the Name of Jesus, said to the stupefied crowd:

My dear Israelites, why this astonishment? The God of
Abraham, the God of Isaac, the God of Jacob, the God of
our fathers, has glorified his servant Jesus, whom you have
handed over and denied before Pilate: he, he had decided
to release him; but you, you denied again and again the
Holy and Just One, going so far as to clamor that the grace
of a notorious murderer be accorded you, while you
pushed on into death him who is the Prince of Life. God
has raised him from the dead; of this we are witnesses…
(Ac 3:12-15, 17).

Peter was imprisoned the same evening for "having announced that in Jesus the resurrection of the dead had arrived"

(Ac 4:2). The next day, having to answer for his action of the previous day, Peter was content to repeat before the Sanhedrin with the same respectful and grave, good-naturedness:

> Leaders of the people and ancients. Let this, therefore, be something well known to all of you and to the whole people of Israel: if this man is here before you, thoroughly healed, it is by the Name of Jesus Christ of Nazareth, whom you have crucified, whom God has raised up (Ac 4:8, 10).

This resurrection was the great experience which had taken hold of the life of Peter, responsible more than anything else for the certitude of his thinking, the incoercible theme of his preaching. When the Sanhedrin forbade him to speak of it, he responded simply: "Judge for yourselves, is it just before God to obey you or God? We, we cannot keep from saying what we have seen and heard" (Ac 4:19-20). As soon as he was released, Peter was back with his young Church. Connecting the present situation to primitive preaching, thus possessing an elevated view of what had happened, they offered together this prayer to God:

> Master, it is you who have made the sky, the earth, the sea and everything there is in it, it is you who have said in the Holy Spirit through the mouth of David your servant and our father:
>
> > Why this tumult of the nations
> > and this vain plotting by the peoples?
> > The kings of the earth have drawn themselves up
> > and the leaders have leagued together
> > against the Lord and against his Christ (Ps 2:1-2).
>
> This is indeed true, they have formed a league in this very town against your holy servant Jesus, Herod, Pontius Pilate, with the nations (of the Gentility) and the peoples of Israel; but he has never ceased to be your Anointed One, and they have only managed to realize the events which your hand and your counsel had decided in advance (Ac 4:23, 24-29).

Some time afterwards, Peter appeared again before the Sanhedrin. This time the High Priest became angry:

"We have explicitly forbidden you," he said to Peter, "to teach in this Name; and behold you have filled Jerusalem with your teaching; and you even pretend to make us responsible for the blood of this man."

"It is better to obey God than men," Peter and the apostles replied. "It is indeed the God of our fathers who has raised up Jesus, him whom you have killed, in hanging him upon wood. It is indeed him whom God has made Head and Savior ..." (Ac 5:27-31).

In the years that followed, a person who had not known Jesus and who had persecuted the primitive Church, was converted from the most rigorous Pharisaism to the purest of Christianity, and he became the apostle Paul. He also presents Jesus in the same fashion as Peter. He shows him to the Jews and to the proselytes as the Savior of Israel and as the coronation of the Revelation of God; he says to them:

> Gentlemen, my brothers, you who are indeed sons descended from Abraham, and you who have mixed with them as men fearing God, it is to us that has been sent the Word of such a salvation. The inhabitants of Jerusalem and their leaders have, in point of fact, scorned this Jesus...; without having found in him the least reason why he should be put to death, they demanded that Pilate have him executed. Nonetheless, after having fully realized everything that had been written about him, they lowered him from his post and laid him in a tomb; but God has raised him from among the dead. He was seen throughout many days by the very ones who had gone up with him from Galilee to Jerusalem; and they are now his witnesses before the people. And we also, we bring you the good news, that which was promised to our fathers and of which they can well declare: God has perfectly fulfilled it in the time of our children, in raising up Jesus, as it is written in the second Psalm:

You are my son
I myself have today begotten you (Ps 2:7).

That God has raised him from the dead to the extent that never again will he return to corruption, He explains in these terms:

I shall grant you the holy things of David, they are assured (Is 55:3).

This, then, is why he also declares in another place:

You will not allow that your Holy One see corruption (Ps 16:10).

David himself, to be sure, after having as long as he lived served the plan of God, fell asleep; he was reunited to his fathers; and he saw corruption. But the One whom God has raised up has not seen corruption. Think well on this then, Gentlemen, my brothers, it is through him that there comes the good news of the remission of sins, and the whole of the justification which you have been unable to obtain through the Law of Moses, in him every believer obtains it (Ac 13:26-39).

The Four Gospels of the Resurrection

To these instances of testimony we could add others. The risen Christ took an unprecedented place in the spirit and in the life of the disciples. Through his resurrection he was consecrated in all of his prerogatives: the Elect of the Divinity, the Head, who had conquered death and who conducted to Life. It was in this atmosphere of triumph that the earliest traditions were established, whence came forth the gospels. We would be within our rights to expect writings of a style elevated to meet the level of the reality; and indeed if they were redacted thirty years or more later, the tone should have been lifted to correspond to the pitch of belief. Now such was not the case: not the least amplification was substituted for, or even added to the simple memory of the original facts. If the most pathetic moments of the Passion have been presented to us from the aspect of minor incidents and practically of miscellaneous happenings, the same is true of the overwhelming event of the Resurrection.

Matthew, the evangelist who has reported the greatest number of wondrous occurrences at the death of Jesus, begins again with relation to the Resurrection: he speaks again of a trembling of the earth; it is he who relates with the most resplendence the apparitions of the angels. Nevertheless, he forms his account with a great deal of tact, as a faithful and circumspect reporter. He has respect for everything that has come to pass, and also respect for what was of a more serious character; he does not insist upon the marvels and, above all, does not consider them as inherent to the event itself; they constitute but the surroundings, the environment.

Concerning the fact strictly speaking, the four gospels respect the secret of God, reserving what there was of the ineffable in the mystery. A Man, who was indeed dead, awakened from the dead, and came back from among the dead. The evangelists do not portray him in majesty nor compose for him a triumphal return. They do not describe the event in an eminent manner, from the point of view of the other world, but modestly, from the viewpoint of here on earth. The witnesses spoke of what they had seen, what they had touched; the writers endeavored to make a part of the thread of human history an incomparable experience which, by its mystery, inevitably escapes the grasp of history.

What had happened to their Master plunged the disciples into mourning and dejection. Even after all that Jesus had said to them, they had no idea of a prompt resurrection. The women, who had been faithful in following him even to his tomb, thought only of enclosing him therein. As for the men, they must have been for the most part immersed in that discouragement attributed by Luke to the two who were returning to their homes on Sunday afternoon (Lk 24:13).

However, we must not exaggerate. It does not seem possible that so many predictions of Jesus as formal and as precise as they were, could have been made for nothing. Several among the disciples, and doubtlessly the greatest of them, must have reflected on them. If their risen Master left them in suspense, it was in order to give them time to think. He would like for the mystery to enter their spirits through an intelligent faith in that which he had said and in that which was written; he will praise this faith several times; he will experience difficulty in creating it in all of them (Jn 20:29). Neither the men nor the women were in the kind of excited frame of mind which would have predisposed them to be overly credulous. They were rather in that state of depression of which Jesus had forewarned them (Mk 14:17; Mt 26:31; Jn 16:20), and which the evangelists did not have the least notion of hiding or of minimizing.

Other traits accentuate still more the discretion of the gospels, and are so many indications of their sincerity. Aside from two more detailed narrations, the apparition along the road to Emmaus in the gospel of Luke (Lk 24:13-32), and the apparition on the banks of the sea of Tiberias in John's gospel (Jn 21:1-23), the accounts are distinguished by their sobriety. They form a single chapter in each of the synoptics, and two in John. Not one of the evangelists pretends to be complete; each of them follows his own information, without conforming to the others. Nowhere does the entanglement and the fragmentary character of their relations become as noticeable as here. John feels it necessary to excuse himself: "Of course," he says, "Jesus performed before his disciples still many other signs which have not been inscribed in this book" (Jn 20:30).

A deception affronts us in the gospel of Mark. To all appearances, he comes to us truncated or unfinished. Might Mark have had the idea of making of the account of the apparitions the debut of another book, as Luke has done at the beginning of the

Acts? Possibly. But the unfinished character could also be explained by other causes, all perhaps fortuitous. The gospel of Mark ends with the first account, the episode of the women before the empty tomb (Mk 16:1-8); the entire conclusion (Mk 16:9-20) appears to come from a different author. Not a thing, of course, precludes this author's having been inspired. As we shall see, he seems to summarize and to ratify what the other evangelists had had the inspiration to recount; he could in this way confirm their authority without adding to the information they give, and without helping to interpret them.

Matthew, for his part, disconcerts us by the abridged twist which he gives to his account. Before the empty tomb, while the guards were stupefied, the women are informed that Jesus is no longer dead (Mt 28:1-7); then they are the first admitted to contemplate the risen Jesus and they carry the news to the disciples (Mt 28:8-10), while the soldiers are paid by the chief Priests to say that the body had been stolen (Mt 28:11-15). As for the men, Matthew acknowledges only the Eleven and is content to indicate that they went to Galilee as Jesus had told them to do, and that there they were favored by a magnificent rendezvous and invested with the great mission (Mt 28:16-20).

Luke, well informed as he usually is about the presence of the women, shows them attentive and active from early in the morning. However, if he gives greater amplitude to their group than Matthew has done, he attributes less importance to their action: they notice that the tomb is empty, they encounter the angels, but do not see Jesus (Lk 24:1-11). Peter also makes the observation (Lk 24:12). Luke next presents the pilgrims from Emmaus: these two men see Jesus; in the course of the account we learn that during the day Peter had also seen Jesus (Lk 24:13-35). Finally, in Jerusalem, the same evening, the Eleven and other disciples enjoy the same favor (Lk 24:36-43); then, as if everything was rushing together, they receive without intermission the final instructions (Lk 24:44-49) and, led towards Bethany, they assist at the Ascension (Lk 24:50-53). It is evident that we have here in curtailed form several tableaux of events relative to the Resurrection.

After Matthew had transmitted only the manifestation in Galilee, after Luke had underlined only the manifestation in Jerusalem, John applied himself to recounting the facts following a more complete pattern. He better expresses the first impressions and the full emotion of the disciples on the day of the Resurrection: their community in mourning, their timidity in the midst of the Jews, their incredulity with regard to the risen Jesus. He gives greater relief to the principal personages, to the Magdalene, to Peter. He describes the states of mind; he allows to be divined the diversity which reigned among them. Above all, he brings into clear perspective the preponderant moments, namely: the empty tomb, the Church hanging in the balance, Jesus finally showing himself. Peter and "the other disciple," who was John himself, both informed by the Magdalene, officially observe that the tomb is empty (Jn 20:1-10). The fact that even the principal disciples, even Peter, were left in suspense, is rendered all the more striking by the singular mission entrusted to Mary Magdalene; this woman who saw Jesus was charged with inviting the disciples to reflection (Jn 20:11-18). Finally, it was only on the evening of that day that Jesus showed himself in Jerusalem to the group of the Eleven, and eight days later in the same place to the most unbelieving among them (Jn 20:19-29).

John was aware of the importance of this initial manifestation in the Holy City. It had reassured the Eleven, and fulfilled the predictions which Jesus had made to them: You will be greatly afflicted at not seeing me, he had said to them; but behold, you will see me again, at the end of much less time than you think; and I also, I shall see you again and I shall place in your hearts a joy which no one ever again can take from you (Jn 16:19, 22). In effect, without much delay, on the very spot where they are still crushed with sadness, the disciples will experience their sadness transformed into joy (Jn 16:20).

The gospel of John could have ended here; and perhaps for

a time it did come to a halt at this point, as would indicate the conclusion which is found there (Jn 20:30). However, to extend still farther the chain of his memories, to avoid giving the impression of forgetting the Galilee of his origins, John has reported with incomparable charm, one of the apparitions of Jesus in this province, a manifestation totally unexpected and deeply intimate, to only a few of the disciples, at the places and in the familiarity of the first encounters, a scene in which Peter is fully rehabilitated and in which John, his friend, is associated to him (Jn 21:1-23). With this astonishing picture there comes to an end, in its actual written form, the gospel of John (Jn 21:24-25).

It is difficult to arrange synoptically the four gospels of the Resurrection. This, nevertheless, is an abridged tableau which one can present of them.

Mk 16

 1-7: women at the empty tomb.
   8: they keep silent.
9-11: Magdalene sees Jesus.
12-13: the two from Emmaus see him.
  14: the Eleven see him.
15-18: The Great Mission conferred.
  19: Ascension of the Lord.
  20: departure and action of the disciples.

Mt 28

 1-8: women and guards at the tomb.
9-10: the women see Jesus.
11-15: the guards reach an understanding with the Jews.
16-17: Jesus seen on a mount of Galilee.
18-20: The Great Mission conferred.

Lk 24

 1-8: women at the empty tomb.
9-11: they give the alert.
  12: Peter makes the observation.

13-33: The two from Emmaus see Jesus.
   34: Peter has seen Jesus.
35-43: the disciples see him.
44-48: Instructions and Mission.
   49: final recommendation.
50-51: Ascension of Jesus.
52-53: joy and prayer of the disciples.

Jn 20

   1: Magdalene at the empty tomb.
   2: they give the alert.
3-10: Peter and John make the observation.
11-18: Magdalene sees Jesus.
19-23: the disciples see him.
   24: Thomas eight days later.
   30: Conclusion of John.
1-14: Jesus seen at the sea of Tiberias.
15-19: destiny of Peter.
20-23: destiny of John.
24-25: Conclusion of disciples.

The Gospel of Paul

A fifth gospel of the Resurrection is offered to us in the first epistle of Paul to the Corinthians. This is perhaps even the most ancient writing which we have on the subject; this fifth gospel might be classified the first. It indicates the manner in which the great event was proposed among the great articles of faith. The passage brings to mind, by its texture and by its importance, that which we read in the same epistle relative to the sacred Supper (1 Cor 11:23-27). Paul writes this about the Resurrection:

> I have transmitted to you, among the teachings of the first order, that which I myself have received, namely: that the Christ died for our sins, according to the Scriptures, then he was placed in the tomb and on the third day he rose, according to the Scriptures. I have also transmitted to you

that he was seen by Cephas, next by the Twelve, and then he was seen at one and the same time by more than five hundred of the brethren, of whom the most part are still living today, although a few have died. Afterwards, in the time that followed, he was seen by James, then by all the Apostles; but in the last place, after everyone else, like a child born out of time, he was even seen by me (1 Cor 15:3-8).

The child born out of time was Paul himself: he referred to himself by this name, and perhaps others gave it to him, because of the exceptional character possessed by his birth to the Christian faith and, still more, by his vocation to the apostolate. The elements which Paul brings under consideration in this tableau are carefully sorted, reduced to the essential, and ultimately formed into two clusters of convincing testimony. He fails to mention, some say, the events of the morning of the Resurrection. This is not completely true; Paul makes it clear enough that the tomb was empty, since he recalls that Jesus had been buried there and that on the third day he was there no longer. If the apparitions to the women are not spoken of, it is because in the matter of official preaching, only the testimony of men was decisive.

Among them, Paul has chosen two of those who were principally responsible for the Christian community, who enjoyed the highest authority in the new society: Peter, or Cephas, the Rock upon whom Jesus had promised that he would build his Church; and James, the Brother of the Lord, the only apostle whom Paul felt himself obliged to see at Jerusalem after having made the acquaintance of Cephas (Gal 1:18-19), and whose kinship with Jesus was worth a privileged situation in the first Judeo-Christian Church (Gal 2:9). These two men are not isolated in their testimony. Along with Cephas, there are the Eleven who had shared the same experience and who formed with him the first teaching Church. Then, as many as five hundred of the brethren had looked upon Jesus in his Resurrection, people whom you could meet, to whom you could speak, Paul says, and who constituted an entire gathering of the Church under instruction.

A bold man is he who would pretend that the Church in its beginnings did not count as many as five hundred members! There were only one hundred and twenty on Pentecost, it is true; but this was in Jerusalem, and the Holy Spirit came unannounced. The assembly in question here is very probably that which gathered in Galilee at the mountain designated by Jesus (Mt 28:16). It does not appear unlikely that five hundred disciples could have been regrouped by him in this province which was his own and in which he had so intensely spent himself!

This then, in resume, is what constitutes, according to Paul, the first set of witnesses to the risen Christ. In the thought of the Apostle, the second comes later and in addition, as the extension of the first. He did not have to furnish the credentials for this one, as he did for the first. Paul, in producing this supplementary sheaf of witnesses, shows that the Christ can always make himself seen, and thus raise up new series of testimony, added to the original series, which is incomparable.

James here is at the head of the procession. Concerning the special apparition, with which he was favored, we can say nothing precise.

As for the apparition to all of the apostles, many commentators are inclined to identify it either with that which is reported by John as having taken place eight days after the Resurrection (Jn 20:26-29), or with that which, according to the last verses of Mark and of the relation of Luke, immediately preceded the Ascension (Mk 16:15-20; Lk 24:44-53; Ac 1:4-9).

This is not a satisfactory interpretation. The apparition to all the apostles, as well as the apparition to Jesus and that to Paul himself, is proclaimed as of a much later date, and lets it be understood that, even after his Ascension, Jesus allowed himself to be seen again for the sake of the development of his Church. The expression "all of the apostles" employed in this case does not designate a specifically determined group, but the principal religious leaders of the primitive Church; one by one, or indeed one day when they were united together, they had seen Jesus.

Finally, in the very last place, and as if lowest in rank among all of these apostles, Paul had also had the singular and unexpected privilege of seeing the Lord! The period of forty days which the first examples of catechesis have attributed to the manifestations and to the experiences is hence found to be extended by Paul.

Aided by these remarks, we are going to resume the evangelical narrations. Our four writers did not have to repeat in writing the word by word summaries which all of the faithful must have known by heart and which formed the rudiments of their religious instruction; in their role as evangelists, they had to illustrate the catechesis through the reciting of the facts which could the best be related to it. These facts, these meager facts, yet facts which revealed so great a mystery, they chose, we have said, with great liberty, each in adopting his own point of view, and in ordering the events according to his inspiration. If, therefore, we wish to observe the rule of entire submission to the texts, it is indispensable that we study each of our evangelists separately, without overly concerning ourselves about making them agree among themselves. The involved character of the redactions will give us a vivid idea of that of the events: the texts will be an image of the facts.

CHAPTER 2

THE EMPTY TOMB

The Tomb is Found Empty

No one saw the Christ free himself of the tomb, nor did anyone say they had seen this. It could be believed that he came forth from the womb of the earth as he came forth from the womb of his mother. It is the thought of the Church that the first revelation which he made of his return to life was to the holy woman who had given him life. Of this manifestation of Jesus to Mary nothing has been passed on: we can say nothing about the time, the duration, or the modality. It was already of an order other than ours, of the transcendent domain in which the Word had become flesh. With his Mother as with God, Jesus found himself in the most profound of his relationships. He unites therein with those who in time and in eternity were the authors of his days. Mary herself, even though she was more advanced than the disciples in the understanding of the mystery, must have received at the Resurrection of her Son an augmentation of light: she found herself more enlightened about the mystery of the Word Incarnate and also more associated to this mystery. The risen Lord "mounted towards his Father," and caused his Mother to make this ascent also. His own Ascension will bring about her Assumption.

He is going to manifest himself to his disciples as if he were still in the midst of them. It was essential that they acquire the experimental certitude, they who had drunk and eaten with him throughout three years, that he was once more alive and remained identically the same. The glory which was his did not truly place him at a distance from them, but allowed him to consecrate himself to them in higher fashion, and to lead them more efficaciously where he himself was going: "I ascend," he can say, "I ascend to my Father and your Father, to my God and to your God" (Jn 20:17).

His disciples were dearer to him than ever: he no longer calls them servants, nor even friends; he calls them his brothers. This is, in fact, the first time in the Gospel that this name is given to them by him: "Go tell my brothers," he directs the first woman who sees him, "that I am going ahead of them into Galilee: there they will see me" (Mt 28:10). "It was again to them," Luke tells us at the beginning of the Acts, "that he presented himself quite alive after his Passion, demonstrating this through many proofs: being seen by them throughout forty days and conversing [with them] on the affairs of the Reign of God."

The first events of the first day gravitate around these two points: the tomb found empty and, at moments, adorned by the apparitions of angels; minds at work, the profound reflection of the greatest disciples. Everything begins with the coming and going of the morning following the feast day. Let us listen to our four evangelists, one after another. We leave to Mark the priority to the degree that he is still able to maintain it; and we place Matthew in parallel.

Mk 16:18

When the Sabbath was over, Mary Magdalene with Mary of James and with Salome had bought spice in view of going to embalm Jesus. And, very early in the morning, the first day of the week, behold, they came to the tomb, indeed at sunrise. And they were saying to one another: "Who will roll the stone away from the entrance to the tomb for us?" But behold, upon looking closely they saw quite distinctly that the stone had been rolled aside. It was, in fact, a very large stone.

Moreover, when they had entered the sepulcher, they saw

a very young man seated to the right, clothed in a white robe; they were stupefied at him. But he declared to them: "Do not be astonished. You seek Jesus of Nazareth the crucified! He has risen, he is no longer here. Behold the place where they laid him. But go now, tell his disciples, Peter particularly, that he precedes you into Galilee; there you will see him, as he has said to you."

At this, they came forth from the tomb and fled, for they were possessed by terror and practically entranced. And they said nothing to anyone, so afraid were they.

Mt 28:1-10

[Jesus was sealed in his tomb and guarded.]

But, after the Sabbath, at the first gleams of light, the first day of the week, Mary Magdalene as well as the other Mary came to inspect the tomb.

And behold, there was a great quake: the angel of the Lord, thundering down from heaven and shaking the earth, had rolled the stone away and was sitting upon it.

His appearance, furthermore, had the brightness of lightning, and his clothing was as white as snow.

Out of the fear that he inspired, the guards were seized with trembling and became as if dead.

But, addressing himself to the women, the angel said to them: "Do not be afraid. For I know that you are seeking Jesus the crucified. He is no longer here, because he has risen, as he said. Come look at the place where he reposed. Then go quickly and tell his disciples this: He has risen from the dead, and behold he precedes you into Galilee; it is there that you will see him. Behold, what I have to say to you."

At this, they promptly left the tomb in a mixture of fear and of great joy, and they ran to carry the news to the disciples of Jesus.

And behold, Jesus met them, and said to them: "Goodday!" But they did not approach except to embrace his feet and to prostrate themselves in adoration before him. In his turn, Jesus declared to them: "Do not be afraid; go, let my brothers know that they have only to take themselves to Galilee: it is there that they will see me."

Let us confront these two accounts, both of which are so lifelike. Each of the narrators writes in his own way, and not according to what his confrere has written. In each gospel we see in movement towards the tomb the same women whom we saw in contemplation there at the time of the deposition of the body: two Marys. The first is always the Magdalene. As for the second, even though she is named Mary of Jose in Mark on Friday evening (Mk 15:47) and Mary of James on Sunday morning (Mk 16:1), she is certainly the same person, designated by her two sons (Mk 15:40). It could be that the evangelist had the intention of emphasizing that the woman who plays an important role at the dawn of the Resurrection is precisely the mother of that James who was a personage of the highest rank in the first Church.

In Matthew, however, this woman has no honor-bearing designation: both times she is called quite simply "the other Mary" (Mt 27:61, 28:1). But, in the spirit of effacement and of humility with which these first Christians were penetrated, such an anonymity was sometimes the equivalent of being singled out; such a way of saying "the other Mary" could very well indicate that this woman was for this account, either directly or through her sons, the one the evangelist referred to. There is no possible doubt about the identity of the person, even in Matthew, since he has written in parallel to Mark that this Mary was the mother of James and of a Joseph who was no other than the Jose of Mark (Mt 27:56=Mk 15:40).

Over and above these two Marys, Mark mentions a third woman whom he names Salome and whom Matthew says was the mother of the sons of Zebedee. At the death of Jesus she was present with the two Marys, according to our two narrators (Mk 15:40; Mt 27:56). At the moment of the entombment, she is no longer mentioned by one or the other, who point out only the two Marys (Mk 15:47; Mt 27:61). Finally, for the preparation of the embalming and the return to the sepulcher, Salome is once more placed with the two Marys, but only in Mark (Mk 16:1) and not in Matthew (Mt 28:1).

These variations between the moments and also between the writers invite us to recognize the complexity of the facts and the guilelessness of the accounts. They confirm the supposition which we have already formulated. These three women were more or less group leaders among all those who were in the service of Jesus. Luke urges us to this interpretation since he designates between the two Marys a certain Joan already encountered as a person of importance (Lk 8:3), and since he explicitly says that these ladies had other women with them (Lk 24:10).

Nothing obliges us to think that they performed together all of the measures that they took; such a banding together would only have attracted to them the attention of the Jews. They must have, on the contrary, set themselves to work in distinct groups, and preserved a certain independence of one another; they dwelled in diverse quarters, did not frequent the same shops, did not have the same trips to make. In supposing, as is rather probable, that they concerted their efforts from Friday evening for the embalming on Sunday morning, it is to be presumed that they had arranged their rendezvous at the tomb and not elsewhere, at dawn of the first day of the week. Only, they did not have clocks with which to determine the hour, nor the same streets to follow in order to be present at the rendezvous.

The sepulcher of Jesus was at the exit of the town, near the Gate spoken of as that of Ephraim or of the Street, whence departed a route for Jaffa. There was there a rather steep ascent, continuing past Golgotha and called Gareb: within only about three hundred yards the rise was over one hundred feet. On the surrounding property and in the gardens there were quarries where it was not difficult to hew out ornate tombs. In order to come out of Jerusalem also in the proximity of the holy sepulcher, there existed at least two other gates. One on the north side of the rampart, called the Gate of Benjamin or of the Fish, was an exit of importance, at the point of departure of three roads, towards Bethany and Jericho to the east, towards Samaria, Galilee and Syria to the north, towards Caesarea to the west. The other gate, on the west side of the rampart, was the Gate of the Gardens, from where there departed the roads in the direction of Jaffa, in the direction of Bethlehem and of Hebron.

The holy women had their choice. There would be no reason for all of them to exit by the same gate. Thus, the separation which I place between them, is not a gratuitous supposition: the text of Luke suggests it; that of John shows us that at the very least Magdalene was in a separate band. Now she is nevertheless named along with the others, and even at the head of the others, by the three synoptics: this is the proof that they present the facts only in curtailed form. That Magdalene is always designated the first among them, and that John even saw fit to limit himself to speaking only of her, is the indication of the great role which she played and of the favored mission which she had to fulfill.

The Observation of the Tomb According to Mark

According to Mark, on Saturday evening, the Sabbath being terminated at the setting of the sun, the women went to the shops to make their purchases of fine oils and of perfumed ointments. According to Luke, they had even begun the preparation of the aromatic substances on Friday evening (Lk 23:56). Their preoccupation was to embalm the body of the Lord in ointments of quality. Mary of Bethany had even endeavored to do this before he had died. This recollection of the recent past was capable of stimulating the zeal of all of them. Matthew alone fails to mention these aromatic substances. The two Marys seated across from the tomb at the moment of the burial (Mt 27:61) come back simply "to contemplate the sepulcher" at dawn on Sunday (Mt 28:1). This evangelist did not dare to write, one might say, that the men had embalmed Jesus, that the women wished to embalm him still better. It is possible that such a complete lack of adaptation with regard to the Resurrection seemed shocking to the writer.

We see them, therefore, on the way to the holy sepulcher through all the gates bordering on each other, these pious women from the following of Jesus, and we know the idea which had set them in motion. It was scarcely daybreak, the sun having just risen; on this point, the three synoptics are in agreement. The expression of which Matthew makes use for this morning is the same which Luke used for Friday evening (Lk 23:54): it was applied then to the first gleams of night, the stars in the sky, the lamps in the houses; it is applied here to the first brightness of dawn. John even says that it was still dark when the Magdalene arrived at the tomb (Jn 20:1). At so early an hour, there were not many people in the street. Whom might one meet outside the walls? Whom in the garden? The women did not realize that the tomb had been sealed during the day on Saturday and that there were soldiers there to guard it. Who would open it for them? Who could move the enormous stone and roll it away from the entry? The women were not able; men were needed, men of strength, with tools and levers. As they made their way at daybreak towards the tomb of Jesus, the women exchanged thoughts of this kind. To the degree that they drew nearer, their uneasiness and emotion increased. For Israelites, for Israelite women, it was a very moving thing to reopen a tomb; and, for fervent disciples, to reopen the tomb of such a Master.

But what was not their astonishment to find the sepulcher gaping open! The account of Mark is so lifelike. Even before being on the spot, the women become aware that the stone had been rolled aside: it was of large dimensions; even at a distance they could see it. Who, then, had been able to anticipate them, to come so soon to open the tomb? Matthew, for his part, no longer speaks of the disquietude of the visitors, no more than he tells what their intention was; he would seem to contradict himself and to be afraid that his reader might not understand. Since there was a guard posted in the garden and seals on the stone, there could be no question of anything having been touched; thus, Matthew is obliged to resume the matter from another point of view. But let us finish the account of Mark, who depicts the situation with inimitable simplicity.

The women make their entrance to the holy sepulcher, not without apprehension, but without difficulty and on one level, it seems. This suggests a spacious tomb with a true sepulchral chamber and perhaps a type of vestibule. On the inside, a very young man (this is the very expression of Mark) was tranquilly seated to the right and lengthily clothed in a white robe. He did not give the impression of being a laborer who would dedicate himself to fatiguing tasks, like that of rolling away the stone or transferring the body. He sat enthroned as a young man honorable in his appearance, the messenger of a mystery. Mark does not even speak of an angel; the women had nevertheless understood that this was one. They are struck not so much by the appearance in which the angel was invested, as by the sight of the empty tomb: they who had so carefully watched where the body had been put (Mk 15:47), observe with stupor that it is no longer there.

The guardian, to be sure, pays them the honor of showing them the chamber, with a courtesy full of attention and reassuring words. He gestures toward the stone ledge on which the body had rested: You seek, he says to them with gentleness, Jesus, your compatriot; the crucified, he adds with tender veneration, by which the women were impressed. In Mark moreover as in Matthew, the term "crucified" is in contrast with that of "risen." The crucified, the angel says, he has risen; his place is no longer here; what you have come to do is no longer needed; but a new office is entrusted to you. Do not remain in your fright; go tell the disciples, Peter above all, that what your Master announced has happened. You would do well to remember what he said to you: "After I have risen, I shall precede you into Galilee" (Mk 14:28; Mt 26:32).

This recollection which the three synoptics reproduce is presented as the promise of friendship. "He will precede you into Galilee" is not enough to say. "He will lead you away into Galilee": he will once more place himself at your head, he will determine the direction of the caravan, as he has done at other times in order to return to your homeland. "It is there that you will see him," that is: that you will see him in tranquillity, many times, quite at your leisure, in the joyful conditions promised for his return (Jn 16:22, 26). The words "He said to you" are repeated, both in Mark and in Matthew, for the return to life (Mt 28:6) as well as for the wondrous new encounter (Mk 16:7).

As reassuring as the address of the angel might have been, the women thought only of hurrying as quickly as possible out of the tomb, and of fleeing. To explain this flight, Mark tells us that they were "possessed by fright and a kind of ecstasy." Their fright was doubtlessly the sacred emotion which had taken hold of them in face of the mystery. But what, then, was this entrancement? It is difficult to exactly determine this. It was probably a kind of bewilderment of spirit in the presence of something which overwhelmed them and transcended them, and which they had not at all expected: they lost their heads. The fear which caused them to flee, also closed their mouths: they did not say anything to anyone. Mark, however, does not say that the silence applied to all of them, nor that it lasted a very long time. Unhappily, the gospel comes to a halt here, and we regret this interruption.

The Observation of the Tomb According to Matthew

We come, therefore, to Matthew. According to him, nature itself paid testimony to the Resurrection as it had borne witness to the death: again the earth trembled. Matthew alone says this, and with as much moderation the second time as the first. He does not intimate that the quake had much of a reverberation; rather, he seems to say that it was not noticed except by those who were then preoccupied with the fate of Jesus. It is not even the signal for the exit from the tomb, but rather the reaction to the coming of the angel; the earthquake was produced by the shock of a messenger from heaven: this angel gave the impression of being like a power of nature.

Mark said nothing of all this; Matthew sees things with more majesty and less familiarity. He is careful not to call the angel a very young man; on the contrary, he names him with solemnity "the angel of the Lord" and portrays him with the characteristics worthy of the vision of an angel: as bright as lightning and as white as snow, all that is the most splendorous in light and in whiteness. These things are traditionally biblical; it was the style. Especially to be noticed about this envoy is his role as the angel of the Lord, for the Lord here is Jesus and the angel is at his service. Nonetheless, he did not come in order to assist the Risen One to come forth from the dead, but to invite the faithful to observe that the tomb was empty, and to help them understand that the Lord had escaped from it.

The first to receive the shock of the angel were the guards. They formed a small post there, four or five men, not habituated to visions, and terrified at the brilliant apparition they had before their eyes: it had caused the earth to tremble, the seals to fly off, the huge stone to roll away. From the moment they gained a bit of control of themselves, they knew that the only thing for them to do was to get out of there, which they did. Matthew tells what followed.

The angel who had dumbfounded the guards applied himself to reassuring the women. There is a more solemn atmosphere here than in Mark, but the conversation is just as familiar; he says the same thing, in the same terms. After this, the text of Matthew separates from Mark's, or, rather, seems to protract it and to complete it. According to Matthew, the women did not fall into the speechlessness of which Mark speaks; they run in order to more quickly carry the news to the men. Matthew indeed says that there was fear on their part, that of being deceived, or of not being believed. But he also says that they were joyful at the thought that the angel had spoken the truth.

How can these differing narrations be reconciled? Is it even necessary to try? Are they not rather in the image of that which happened? Is it even a question of the same women? Is it a matter of the same hours? Can one believe that, before this unexpected marvel, these holy women had all adopted the same attitude? Is it characteristic of women to be found so easily in accord? The greatest of the disciples will be divided in their sentiments. How can we think that the women would not be? If at first some of them did not speak, is it possible that they could restrain themselves very long? They must have, in what followed, chimed in with the others, and lost every trace of fear. Matthew says so briefly; Luke will also say so; and Mark, possibly, would have related more details if his account was not cut off here; the author of the final verses has not filled this gap.

According to the continuation of the account of Matthew, the women along the road they hastily traversed were favored with an apparition of the Risen One. This is recounted with simplicity. Jesus, so to speak, barred their way: this sudden encounter was startling, but the Lord gave to it a comely twist. He did not act ostentatiously toward these good ladies: Rejoice, he said to them: which was a cordial fashion of wishing them good-day. It is impossible to imagine a simpler presentation, one more distant from all mystification: Jesus was there, and it was so certainly he, that one could not fail to recognize him. But, to find him again so much alive after having seen him so terribly dead was overwhelming; also it is comprehensible that there is such a contrast between them and him: if he did not make a show of things, they felt that they had to do so. We see them prostrated with fervor and adoration! Nevertheless, he begs them not to be afraid, and not to delay, but to go to tell those whom he tenderly calls his brothers that he would rendezvous with them in Galilee. This account confirms that the women were messengers of the Resurrection.

This simple apparition to the women, which assuredly is of great beauty, all the same remains rather vague, being presented as a kind of parenthesis in Matthew's account. One would say that the evangelist was unwilling to omit it, but also unwilling to make it completely precise. At the dawn of the Resurrection, it was not to the disciples that the Lord first showed himself, but to the women: it was just that the memory of this be consigned. Matthew however speaks of the matter in general terms, and it is quite possible that he attributes to the entire group of women what happened to only one of them. He was rather accustomed to this procedure; the last example we had was that of the robbers insulting Jesus on the Cross (Mt 27:44). The apparition recounted here could, therefore, not be different from that with which the Magdalene was favored. In this respect, John will put things in their exact perspective by revealing the singularity of a favor which Matthew has left to the collectivity: in reality, one woman alone saw Jesus first, and this was the Magdalene. For Matthew it was premature to write this. Magdalene herself, a source of information, could have requested that her name not be spoken. The features of the account in Matthew agree with those of John's account.

Still other reasons make us think that Jesus appeared first of all to Magdalene alone. The first place which is attributed to her by all the synoptics, and by Matthew himself. The fact that Luke, in his summary of the events of the morning, presents the women as having seen some angels but not the Lord (Lk 24:3-10), and that, in the episode of the disciples of Emmaus, he reports simply this: "Some women of our group ... saw an apparition of angels, who said he was alive" (Lk 24:22-23). Finally a last confirmation, the author of the last verses of Mark says expressly that Mary of Magdala was the first to see the risen Jesus (Mk 16:9). If, however, the apparition presented by Matthew was really an apparition to an entire group of women, then it is fitting to situate it in the earliest morning hours, without being able to say at what spot, in the garden, in the town or in some house.

The guards bribed by the priests

Before coming to the summarized account of Luke and the detailed account of John, we must first finish with that of Matthew in what is related to the happenings of the morning and the observation of the tomb. There were, according to Matthew, other witnesses: these were the guards. He is not less informed about them than about the women, and sets them in parallel with each other. At the same time when the women are going to make their announcement to the disciples, and especially to Peter (Mk 16:7), the guards go to make their report to their patrons, the chief Priests, by whom they were at that moment employed. The two embassies overlap one another in the tableau, as if the women and the soldiers had met at the gates of the town and not exactly at the tomb.

> As they were on the way, behold, several of the guards came to the town to announce to the chief Priests everything that had happened. The latter, after having assembled with the Ancients, and after having deliberated, gave an appreciable sum of money to the soldiers, in recommending to them: "Say this: His disciples came during the night to steal him away while we were sleeping. When the matter reaches the ears of the governor, we shall assure him that you were not at fault." As for them, they took the money and repeated the story which they had been instructed to tell. This is why this account was spread among the Jews and is still current today (Mt 28:11-15).

Matthew did not invent this piece of history. He is the only one who tells it, perhaps because he was the only one to be well informed about it. It does not seem that it held much importance in the eyes of the disciples: several, no doubt did not learn about it until later on; it appeared to them to be no more than an aside. The soldiers were not posted in the garden until during the day of Saturday, and in the early hours of Sunday they left the place. Matthew makes it understood that the chief Priests, because of their embarrassment, felt the need of consorting with the Ancients. What's this, the affair of this Jesus of Nazareth is still not finished then? Behold, it resurfaced once more, and in the most subtle fashion, which would be the most perilous because the most elusive; the success of the Galilean could begin again and be amplified, favored by a so-called resurrection. It was exactly this imposture which the Jewish leaders feared and which they had desired to prevent (Mt 27:64). Placed before strange facts, they do not seek the true nature of them, they merely dread their consequences.

If everything had been upset in the garden, if the seals had been removed, if the tomb was empty, where could the body be found? What should be done? These soldiers who had been unable to keep an efficacious watch, were soldiers of Rome; they had only been loaned to the Jewish authorities. It was not possible to do away with them; to have them punished would cause them to talk. The best thing to do would be to pay them well in order to obtain their silence, and to permit the accreditation of the rumor of a theft of the body by the disciples. But what if the Governor came to know about the thing, and became angry at a service badly rendered? Don't let that worry you, the Jews say; we shall appease him and cover up for you. The essential thing, as far as the directors were concerned, was to make a part of public opinion the idea which had come to their imaginations; the disciples had found a means to steal the body. Such is the explanation that was propagated, in the town and in the countryside, among the Israelites who remained rebellious to the Gospel of the Resurrection. Matthew makes the observation that at the moment when he was writing, this was still what was said in the Jewish milieux.

The Observation of the Tomb According to Luke

We see now, such as it is taken up once more and summarized by Luke, the account of these initial observations of the tomb.

The holy women, who were so concerned about embalming the body of Jesus, nevertheless observed the Sabbath rest throughout the day, according to the commandment.

But, then the first day of the week, at the first streak of dawn, they came back to the sepulcher, carrying the aromatic substances which they had prepared. Now, they found the stone rolled away from the tomb. But, when they had entered, they no longer found the body of the Lord Jesus. There they were, not knowing what to make of this affair, when two distinguished men presented themselves to them in dazzling costume. All of them were seized with fright and lowered their faces to the earth; but they addressed the women: "Why do you seek the living among the dead? He is not here, he has risen. Recall how he spoke to you when he was still in Galilee, when he said of the Son of Man: he must be delivered into the hands of sinners, and be crucified, and the third day rise."

They, in fact, called to mind the words which he had spoken. And, having returned from the tomb, they announced all of these things to the Eleven as well as to all the others. Now, these women were Mary Magdalene, and Joan and Mary of James, and the others who were with them. They reported these things to the apostles. Still, it seemed to the latter that such words proceeded from delirium, and they did not believe the women.

Nevertheless, Peter arose and ran to the tomb. Upon bending down in order to look in, he saw that there was no longer anything there except the strips of cloth. Then he went back to his house, in great astonishment at what had happened (Lk 24:1-12).

The final remark set aside, Luke does not tell us very much which we didn't already know. More than any of the other evangelists, he singles out the emptiness of the tomb; if the women were the first to observe it, the men do so in their turn: Peter comes to see (Lk 24:12); others also (Lk 24:24). Upon their entry into the sepulchral chamber, the women seeing that the body is no longer there are at first completely nonplussed, and do not know what to think. Only after this do they find themselves in the presence of two messengers: by the brilliance and the suddenness of the apparition, they understand that these are angels.

The description given by Luke is on middle ground between Mark's and Matthew's: it is less simple than the former,
but is not as thunderous as the latter; on the other hand, Luke
does not have merely one angel, as Mark and Matthew do; he
mentions two, as does John (Jn 20:12). Men today are not particularly favorable toward such visions; since in their experience they have not met any angels, they conclude that there are
none in all the great universe. But, at the time of Jesus, all of the
Israelites, outside of the more flighty of the Sadducees, were
convinced of the existence of angels and the past of their religion
was peopled with pure spirits. To be sure, the vision of an angel
remained quite an extraordinary thing to them, and most often
inspired in them a sacred fear; but it never seemed impossible to
them, and ordinarily they had no difficulty in recognizing, beneath the form in which he was clothed, the messenger of the
invisible world. The angels at the tomb of Jesus are no more
amazing than the angels at his crib; in both cases, their service is
of the same sort.

According to our gospels, no one is inclined at any time to
confuse or to place on the same level of reality the demonstrations of the Risen One and the apparitions of the angels. The
latter simply furnish an admirable adornment of this radiant
morning of the Resurrection. They brighten with their presence
the gloom of the funereal cavern, they are the guardians of the
empty chamber, and above all they are through their affable instruction the heralds of the mystery, they prepare the Church to
believe. The women alone see them. Peter and John observe that
the tomb is empty, that attentive servants had been at work there,
but they do not see the angels. The holy women were favored
with the vision perhaps because they were better disposed for it
than the men, and especially because they had as their mission
the continuation of the role of the angels and the preparation of
the Church for the faith. This vision offers, in the text of Luke,
something gently revealing, which is proper to this evangelist.

On this illustrious day, the women were in effect messengers of the mystery. The whole text of Luke proclaims this with a delicate openness which has not been sufficiently noticed. If in several features it seems to be an abridgement of the two which had preceded it, in still more aspects it denotes information of the first order. It is full of lived experience: for example, the attitude of the women who were so troubled by the sight of the empty tomb; these figures bent to the earth before the two luminous faces which filled the sepulcher with their brightness. The account is equally vibrant with declarations full of implied meaning, like the reproach for seeking the Living among the dead, and the reminder of what was spoken in the early days in Galilee.

There is, throughout this narrative, an accentuated note of feminine inspiration, of feminine pride: these women were of an open spirit and an intelligent zeal. The debut of the message addressed to them is of the greatest beauty. What follows, starting with "Recall how...", is less striking and is but a reminder of the past. As Luke does not intend to speak of Galilee in his gospel of the Resurrection, the message reported does not tell the disciples that the Lord will see them again in Galilee, but only asks them to remember what he had said to them when he was with them in Galilee. Luke is a writer quite aware of all these nuances.

The women who received the message did in fact remember. The rapprochement of the words formulated by the angels with those which Jesus had said put them on the right track. They repeated all of these things to all of the men of their little society (Lk 24:22). "All of these things," that is, what they had seen, what the angels had said, and what Jesus had foretold. All the same, was it true that he had already arisen from the dead? Since he had said that this would be, why not believe that it had already happened? The women, this morning, being more prudent than the men, the Lord made use of them in order to forewarn "his brothers" and to lead them to believe even before to see (Jn 20:29); and it was not a question of only the greatest ladies, but of all those who accompanied them. With surprising unanimity they all said the same things to all of the disciples whom they met; they insisted hardily, even among those who had the title and quality of Apostles. They were the apostles of the Apostles.

The principal ones are named by Luke only at the end of the account and when they have, so to speak, reached the end of their role. They are as ever the two Marys, that of Magdala, and the mother of James, as in Mark and in Matthew. Luke inscribes between these two names that of Joan, which in a way replaces that of Salome, whom Mark has placed third in the trio which he also presents. This Joan, already counted by Luke among the number of the friends of Jesus (Lk 8:3), was a great lady of Galilee, the wife of the steward of Herod, the tetrarch of this country; she was one of those who had followed the Master from Galilee (Lk 23:49, 55). If Luke sets her in a place of honor in this relation of the events of Sunday, possibly it is because it was to her he owed this relation. We might also ask ourselves why Luke, who is so well informed concerning the role of the women, leaves Magdalene with the others, while John allows for her a place apart; there is no answer to this, except perhaps that Magdalene herself prevented her being put in the limelight.

The men showed themselves rebellious to the information brought in by the women, as well as to their suggestions. Luke even says that they treated all this as the product of delirium and they had no faith in it. Luke amplifies and generalizes: to augment the role of the women, he disparages the attitude of the men. All were not as close-minded as he would appear to indicate. The two whom he will show us along the route to Emmaus will admit to being troubled by what the women had said (Lk 24:22). And if, according to Luke himself, Peter arose to run to the tomb, this is indeed the proof that he did not take everything for delirium. Peter was the first among the men to verify that the tomb was empty. He came to it forewarned by the women. He observed, upon bending down with due respect, that if the tomb was empty, it did not give the impression of having been violated; and it did not appear that the body had been stolen, since the strips of cloth were still there. Peter was greatly astonished. He went back, not to his brothers, but to his home, to the house in which he was a guest. He needed to be alone. He needed to reflect. Luke, in his summary tableau, leaves us with this view of Peter.

CHAPTER 3

PETER AND MARY MAGDALENE

Peter Makes the Observation, According to John

John returns to this same tableau, with more details. In order to do this, he has to retrace the entire account of the events of the morning. He is well qualified to speak of the matter, since he was personally involved in it, along with Peter whom he scarcely left, and whom he sustained in his grief. Peter was perhaps twice as old as John; but they were very close friends of one another: their common love for Jesus was the bond which united them. Let us listen, then, to the report of the last gospel, with all of its circumstances.

Jesus had been entombed in the very garden where he had been crucified: he could not be carried farther, because of the Sabbath.

But the first day of the week, Mary Magdalene arrived at the sepulcher, early in the morning, when it was still dark. She saw then that the stone had been taken away from the sepulcher. Running, therefore, she came to Simon Peter and to the other disciple, the one whom Jesus loved, and she declared to them: "They have taken the Lord from his tomb, and we do not know where they have put him." Of course, Peter went forth, the other disciple also. Thus, they betook themselves to the tomb, in fact they ran, both of them together. Only, the other disciple ran in front, more quickly than Peter, and he reached the tomb first. And stooping down, he plainly saw lying on the ground the strips of cloth. Nonetheless, he did not enter. Then Simon Peter who was following him also arrived. He went into the tomb. He, in his turn, contemplated the cloth strips lying on the ground. He contemplated, besides, the shroud-like cloth which had been wrapped around the head of Jesus: this piece of linen was not lying with the bands of cloth, but was set aside, well folded up in a certain spot. Then the other disciple also entered, the one who had arrived at the tomb first. He saw, he believed. They had not yet, in effect, understood through Scripture that it must be that Jesus rise from among the dead. These disciples, therefore, went back again to their dwelling (Jn 20:1-10).

This account bears the customary signature: "the disciple whom Jesus loved." Still, the verb "love" employed here is the common term and not the studied form which is found in the other passages (Jn 13:23, 21:20); if this difference has a meaning, it is difficult to tell what it is.

We are struck first of all by the role given to Mary Magdalene. The synoptics had already placed her first among the women: John himself sets her totally apart. He attributes privileges to her which seem to be reserved to her alone. This is not to say that she was by herself so early in the morning going through the streets and gardens. "We do not know where they took him," she says to Peter and to John; this plural makes it clear that she did not venture to the tomb alone. She had her little group also, just like the mother of James, the wife of Zebedee, the wife of Chusa could have had theirs.

What John wishes to tell us is that Mary Magdalene arrived first at the holy sepulcher, even before sunrise, and also that she was alone in running to seek the two disciples in order to bring them to the tomb, and alone in remaining there after they had gone back. But nothing excludes the possibility that Mary Magdalene, who is presented as a person of significance, had constantly with her, in the measures she took, several of her friends; she alone counted for the narrator, the others only followed or served.

Yet, someone in this episode was a considerably greater personage than Mary Magdalene, and this was Simon Peter. His failure had not caused him to forfeit his rank. It was to him that they recurred when it was a question of seeing to the interests of the Lord Jesus. Simon Peter was with John, perhaps at the home where John was staying, when the Magdalene came to notify them. If Zebedee possessed a place of lodging in Jerusalem, it was at the disposal of his sons and their companions: Peter was the guest of his friend.

The entire episode is replete with hurried movement: all the parties concerned are seen racing to and fro. Simon Peter possibly was not far from being forty years old, he no longer had the quickness nor the youth of John; but how these men move in their rush towards the tomb of their Master! There is, in the text, a mingling of verbs in the past, the present and the imperfect, which reminds us of the most spirited sections of the gospel of Mark. The verbs in the past naturally express the acts which involved hurry; the imperfects and the presents, the attitudes in which one tarries.

Peter, having entered the chamber hastily and recklessly, remained there full of thought, contemplating what he saw: the strips of cloth on the ground in such a fashion that they could even be seen without entering, the shroud folded and arranged, and set to the side. This shroud-like cloth which John says was put about the head of Jesus (Jn 20:7) must have been the splendid winding sheet, purchased by Joseph, an ample piece of material in which the whole body had been enveloped and which had been wrapped around the head; it was nothing more now than a precious package in the holy sepulcher.

Also to be noted is the respect of John for the person of Peter. The disciple whom Jesus loved effaces himself before Simon, as one does before someone greater than himself, as one does before his chief. This is not merely a question of age and of precedence; there is something else here. John is full of regard for Peter, because it belonged to Peter to see and to act: Peter was the one responsible. John did not at first enter the holy sepulcher. He did not enter until after his friend, and probably at the request of the latter. He then assisted in the examination which Peter made of everything; but he did not intervene, he respected the silence of his chief. This possesses both greatness and beauty. These two men do not even exchange their impressions: they are in the presence of a mystery, a light begins to dawn in their spirit.

John confesses that it was at this moment that he believed. He asks pardon for only having done so at this moment! Doubtlessly, he believed even before having seen Jesus, but nevertheless not before having seen the empty tomb and the array of the cloths used to wrap the dead: this was already too much, it betrayed a slowness to believe, it would have been more perfect to adhere to the divine mystery uniquely upon the word of God. Scripture, he thought, contains everything necessary in order to put us on the right path; but we have not understood Scripture; none of us conceived of a Messiah triumphing through suffering and returning so soon from the abode of the dead.

Neither what had been written, nor what Jesus himself had said, had sufficiently prepared the disciples to be witnesses of the mystery; yet true faith could not be formed except at this price. Jesus had no desire to force the spirit, to obtain from his disciples a constrained faith, like that which imposed itself upon the demons, or which he would extort from the Jews if he encamped before their Sanhedrin in the freshness of his Resurrection. He desired an intelligent and free adhesion, a reflective and penetrating faith, cordial, generous and profoundly thought out, a faith which would not stop at the Man, but which would go as far as God. This is the reason for which he left his disciple in suspense, and even the first among them, until the middle, indeed even until the end, of this the "third day" after his death. Quite discreetly John makes it known to us that this faith was granted to him at the moment in which he effected with Peter the more or less official inspection of the tomb. At the end Peter and he went back side by side, and in silence.

What was Peter thinking? He was astonished, Luke says, and we could just as well translate "struck with wonder": at the thing which had happened and which was for him anything but an ordinary matter (Lk 24:12). John does not resolve anything as to the intimate thought of Peter, but he gives proof of such a respect for his great brother that one can hardly suppose that the reflection of Peter was less advanced than that of John.

Peter appears to us from the point of view of faith, as in the brightness of a dawn. We see him setting out into the light but lost in the mystery. It does not enter his mind that hostile hands could have carried off the body of Jesus. He was firmly convinced that death had relaxed its grip, and that the Holy Servant of Yahveh was no longer the prey of the tomb or of Sheol. He told himself that the Lord God must have taken back to himself his beloved Son. With the usual dispatch of his spirit, Peter must have begun to believe that Jesus was "seated at the Right of the Father." Peter was ahead of the event. Nevertheless, the affair was too serious for him to be able to speak of it to his brothers. This is why he remained silent. But he believed. Thus, when Jesus appears to him in the course of the day, this will not be in order to lead him to believe, but to signify to him: I have not yet ascended, but I ascend to my Father and your Father. And thus will the faith of Peter be guided into an exact view of the situation.

The Magdalene Sees Jesus

We continue in our reading of John's gospel.

[The disciples, Peter and John, returned then to their dwelling.]
But Mary remained. She remained very near to the tomb, outside of it, and all in tears. Still weeping, she bent down towards the interior of the tomb. It was then that she perceived the two angels in white: they were seated, one at the head and the other at the foot of the place where the body of Jesus had lain. Then they said to her: "Woman, why do you weep?" She answered them: "Because they

have taken away my Lord and I do not know where they
have laid him."
When she had said this, she turned partly around. Then
she perceived Jesus standing there; only, she did not know
that it was Jesus. "Woman, why are you weeping?" Jesus
asked her. "Whom do you seek?" She, thinking that he
was the guardian of the garden, said to him: "Sir, if it was
you who moved him, tell me where you have laid him
and I shall go to take care of him." Jesus said to her:
"Miriam!" She, having completely turned towards him,
said to him in Hebrew: "Rabboni!" which means: "My
Master!" Jesus said to her: "Do not cling to me, for I have
not yet ascended to the Father; but go to my brothers, and
tell them: I ascend to my Father and your Father, my God
and your God." Mary Magdalene went in fact to announce
to the disciples: "I have seen the Lord!" and those things
which he had said to her (Jn 20:11-18).

There is not, in this account, the least trace of skillful ar-
rangement, but on the contrary a certain awkwardness which
portrays rather well the entangled nature of the situation. This
Mary Magdalene, called more familiarly Mary, strikes the figure
of a soul in pain. Peter and John have departed, profoundly stirred
in their thoughts. She stubbornly remains there, in the antecham-
ber if there was one, quite near to the tomb, neither completely
outside nor totally inside. She wept warm tears, out loud, like a
woman in terrible grief who no longer very well knows what
she is saying or what she is doing. Her spirit was not orientated
toward the resurrection. The two close friends of Jesus had left
without saying anything. The angels do not say anything either
which might have enlightened her: her sadness kept her from
reflecting and made her moan and talk too much. She did not
dare to enter the sepulchral chamber but leaned over to look in.
It was to this hollow of the tomb that her eyes returned in tears.
    The two angels whom she beheld there were indeed, to
John's way of thinking, the two messengers of the account of
Luke (Lk 24:4); but Mary sees them according to the shade of her
disposition, without the splendor signaled by Matthew (Mt 28:3),

and more prosaically than is written in Mark (Mk 16:5). They are seated on the ledge where Jesus had lain, one at the head, the other at the foot, and she takes them for two men who had taken up the body and transferred it. Then, scarcely had they addressed her in terms full of deference and condolence: "Woman, what are you weeping for?", when she turned aside, as if now she was looking for someone behind her. On this occasion the Magdalene is no longer an assuaged contemplative; she is no longer anything but a sensitive and tormented heart. For the moment she is plunged into her darkness; she will receive no light except from Jesus himself.

Half turned towards the outside as she was, Mary perceived another silhouette. The evangelist does not manage to produce an adequate redaction. He means to say that this new silhouette must not have had in the eyes of Mary the strangeness of the preceding ones. For it was no longer a question of a borrowed means of figuration, as for the two beings in the heart of the holy sepulcher, but of the reality itself of Jesus: it was he who was there, in front of his tomb. Mary will be able to throw herself at his feet, to touch them; she will recognize him. But now, unhappily, she sees him through her tears and the deformation of her disturbed thoughts, she has the fixed notion of the body's having been stolen. She believes that this man is the gardener of the distinguished Joseph of Arimathea; the transfer could certainly not have been made without the gardener's having known it. And here he is, addressing himself to her, also with a great deal of deference, as one speaks to a great lady.

She responds to him on the same tone, as one would do to a gentleman of importance. "Sir," she says to him, in order to utter to him, it is true, insensate things: "Tell me where you have put him, and I shall take him." She imagines that if the body had been relocated, it was not properly attended to. Who knew where it had been put, and if it was decently buried? She says that she will take charge of this! Did she even know how she would go about this? Such remarks betray the state of the person and reflect the situation.

Then Jesus makes himself known to the first person whom he allowed to see him in the Resurrection. The evangelist once more finds the inimitable gift which he has for painting such scenes in the simple grandeur which characterized them. The Lord speaks but one word, the name of friendship, that which he used when he was the guest of Mary and when she listened so well to his lessons. John has the delicate touch to write this name in the very language in which it was uttered. Jesus must have articulated it in a manner to render quite recognizable the ring and intonation of his own voice; no doubt he even added a little bit to his accent as if to affirm in the tones of an affectionate reproach: "Miriam! how long will you search for the Living among the dead?" This appeal deals a triumphant *coup de grace*. Surprised at hearing herself called by her own name and on this tone, Mary finishes by turning all the way around, with a start of her entire body. It was clear as day, her Master was before her. She also speaks to him as previously, not by the more striking name, but by the title which could be considered as very affectionate and very deferential, that which she proffered in intimacy: "Rabboni," she said. In Hebrew, the evangelist ingenuously writes; that is: in Aramaic, in the tongue which they spoke among themselves. John takes the trouble to translate that Rabboni signifies Master. But the word here dons a nuance of great respect; it is of those which can be addressed to God himself.

Mary was stirred by the instincts of her heart and by the inspirations of the Spirit. Spontaneously she responds to friendship with friendship. Nevertheless, the majesty of the event does not escape her. At the same time that she speaks to Jesus so tenderly and so worthily, Mary throws herself to the ground at his feet and she embraces them. This gesture is not described by John, but the words which he reports presuppose it. These words are only explicable, however, if we attribute to the gesture the sense of an act of adoration quite distant from any kind of sentimentality. Doubtlessly, the profession of Mary does not have the greatness of that which will soon redeem the incredulous

Thomas: "My Lord and my God" (Jn 20:28); but it is exactly this that she thinks as she prostrates herself before her "Rabboni."

He consents that she remain there a moment, and this moment of grace suffices to transform Mary. To seize and to contemplate Jesus in his glory as she does on this radiant morning, was to recognize that he was everything that he had said, it was to confess that he is God. If she made the gesture of "clinging to" him, it was not in the way that one might be attached to the most loved and venerated of men, but as one must cling to God. Suddenly brought back to reality, cured of all agitation, reestablished in her serenity, she goes to the very heart of the mystery, she is capable of adoring in spirit and in truth.

It is only on this condition that the declaration of Jesus can be understood well. He says to her: "Do not cling to me like this, for I have not ascended to my Father." There is assuredly mystery in these two propositions, and as much in the first as in the second; but the mystery of the second throws light upon that of the first. The Lord means to say to the woman adoring him: If I had fully returned to my Father, you might thus attach yourself to me: for the moment this is premature; I still have to show myself to my brothers, go tell them that I am in my Ascension. And, this Ascension, Jesus describes to Mary in simple and inimitable terms which recall other declarations of his: I am no longer of this world, I ascend to my Father (Jn 14:3, 28; 17:5, 13 and elsewhere); but my Father is also your Father, and my God your God; where I go you will come, where I am you will also be with me (Jn 14:23, 17:24).

Such words entrusted to the Magdalene are the indication that the adoration of this woman was allied to the Divinity more than to the Humanity of the "Rabboni." To fail to see this is to miss what is essential in the report of John; to see it furnishes the key to the astonishing primacy which the synoptics and all tradition have attributed to the Magdalene in the gospel of the Resurrection.

John concludes his relation in a categorical manner and with solemnity: It was in fact this woman, he writes, "it was

Mary the Magdalene, who went to announce to the disciples: 'Indeed, I have seen the Lord!' And also," John adds rather awkwardly, "what he had said to her." The evangelist wishes to make it understood that Magdalene acquitted herself perfectly of her mission. She did not content herself with relating the fact: He has risen, I have seen him. She faithfully reported the words which were spoken, as profound as they were: He spoke to me, this is what he said. If we bring all of these features together, we grasp more clearly the nature of the grace accorded to this woman, and what role she had to play. This role had already been intimated by the other evangelists; it was the desire of John to expose it more distinctly and even to explain it.

The author who has written the final verses of Mark has himself registered the grandeur of the privilege reserved to the Magdalene, in recalling the way in which she had first been privileged. He thus summarizes the first apparition:

"Risen upon the morning of the first day of the week, he appeared first to Mary, the Magdalene, from whom he had expelled seven demons. She went to carry the good news to those who had been with him. Yet they, even after having heard that he was alive and that he had been seen by her, did not believe" (Mk 16:9-11). We know through Luke that Magdalene had been the prey of a great many devils (Lk 8:2). We have learned through John that she had been the first to see Jesus on Sunday morning. This does not mean that this brief closing fragment was merely borrowed from Luke and from John. Magdalene being known in the Churches, someone could have had the inspiration to make it a part of Scripture that this woman who had received the singular favor of the first apparition of Jesus had come back from a great distance spiritually, and that she was an illustrious convert of the Lord's.

Finally, it must be remarked, the apparition to the Magdalene, such as it is recounted by John, presents the same characteristics as the apparition to the women which is related in Matthew (Mt 28:9-10). The same prepossessing demonstration on the part of Jesus, the same prostration in adoration on the part of the women who see him. If it is a question of the same scene, as is possible, then the identification of the tableau follows quite naturally. If it is a matter of two scenes succeeding one another in the course of Sunday morning, it means that Jesus manifested himself to these holy women in a somewhat similar manner and that the same kind of inspiration dictated to them the same gestures which were, for that matter, quite feminine at the same time as very religious. The Lord, gently, brings their manifestation to an end: Do not cling to me... "go to my brothers," he says in the account of Matthew just as in that of John (Mt 28:10; Jn 20:17). The apparitions to the men, we note, will be in quite another fashion: "Do not touch me," Jesus says to Magdalene (Jn 20:17); "Touch and see," he says to the men (Lk 24:39). The experiences, to be sure, do not have the same object. Mary already willed to take hold of God; this is why Jesus said to her: Not immediately. The disciples hesitated in rediscovering the Man; this is why Jesus said to them: Do so then, quickly!

Even if the apparition to the women, which we have read in Matthew, is none other than the apparition to Magdalene, of the message confided Matthew has kept only the part which was the most accessible to his ordinary readers. Magdalene was in effect assigned to announce to the disciples that the Lord would see them again and reserved for them further sensible attentions; but she was also charged to tell them that he was in his ascent to God. The terrestrial part of the message remained intelligible to a greater number; the other part, which was completely celestial, could reach only the souls of the elite.

It is our opinion that even at the moment the Ascension concludes, all will not yet be equally prepared to comprehend it (Ac 1:67), even though Jesus has forewarned them of the grandeur of the event: "What will it be then, if you see the Son of Man ascending where he at first was?" (Jn 6:62). It is not astonishing that Magdalene, having had to remind the brethren of this lofty aspect of the mystery, experienced trouble in making herself heard. According to the final verses of Mark, she was no better heard when she testified that Jesus was indeed alive (Mk. 16:10;

Jn 20:18), than according to the gospel of Luke were the other women when they affirmed that they had seen angels who watched over the empty tomb and had told them the same thing (Lk 24:11).

The men were truly slow to believe and Jesus will most certainly have good reason to reproach them for their incredulity and their hardness of heart (Mk 16:14). The concurrence of circumstances, the convergence of testimony, the observation of the empty but unviolated sepulcher, which they had every opportunity to make during the day, all of this ought to have opened "the eyes of their heart." For some, John has told us, these things were in fact decisive. But, for the most part, the disciples remained in the state of spirit described by the lengthy account in which Luke makes way for several incidents of the memorable day.

THE ROAD TO EMMAUS

The Two Disciples from Emmaus See Jesus

Certain men see Jesus. Before the conclusion of the day, Peter himself will have seen Jesus, and he will have called together his brothers in order to tell them. This great page of the gospel of Luke must be read in its entirety.

Then, everything that the women might have said, was drivel as far as the disciples were concerned.

Now that same day, two among them were on the road to a village which was located at sixty stadia from Jerusalem, the name of which was Emmaus. And they chatted between themselves about everything that had happened. Now it came to pass while they chatted and discussed in this way, that Jesus in person, having joined them, accompanied them along the road. But their eyes were rendered powerless to recognize him. He said to them: "What have you been talking about as you walked?" At this, they came to a halt with an air of sadness. One of them, who was named Cleopas, nonetheless began to speak to him: "Have you been so alone in your sojourn in Jerusalem that you don't even know what has happened during the last few days?" "And what is this?" he asked of them. "Ah, the affair of Jesus of Nazareth," they answered him. "He was a man of renown, a prophet, mighty in works and in words, in the regard of God and of the whole people... Consequently, our ruling Priests and our leaders delivered him to be condemned to death and had him crucified. Yet we, we hope that it is he who is to deliver Israel... But, what is certain is that today is the third day since all of this began... To be truthful, some of the women of our group have set us astir. Having gone to the sepulcher very early in the morning and not having found his body, they came to say that they had even had a vision of angels, and that they affirmed he is alive... Also, several of our companions went out to the sepulcher and indeed they found it in the condition described by the women; but, him, they did not see."

It was then that he said to them: "Ah! how spiritless you are, and how slow your heart is to believe everything the prophets have said! Did not the Christ have to suffer all this in order to enter into his glory?" On this point, beginning with Moses and going through all of the Prophets, he interpreted for them throughout Scripture all that was related to himself.

They thus drew near the village where they were going. Then he gave the impression of going on. But they forcefully insisted that he remain, saying: "Stay with us, for evening is near, and the day is already far gone." In point of fact, he went in to remain with them. And behold what happened when he sat at table with them: he took the bread and uttered the blessing, then, breaking it, he distributed it to them. Then, at last, their eyes were opened, and they recognized him perfectly... But he had disappeared from before them... They therefore said to each other: "Were not our hearts burning within us when he spoke to us along the road and unveiled the Scriptures to us?" And, at that very hour, they arose and turned back to Jerusalem (Lk 24:13-33).

We should notice in this account the finesse of spirit and artfulness of writing. It is a page as polished as the most beautiful of the Greek Bible. If Luke selected this apparition in preference to others, it is no doubt because he was well informed about it, and also by reason of the reverberation it must have had among the faithful, because of its originality; and finally, because it represented an entire situation. These two disciples, most assiduous in following Jesus, had been convinced that he was the Christ. They were not disciples of a recent date; possibly they were recruits from the first year of the ministry. At the time when Jesus circulated across Judea, he could have come into their small region, attracted them through his influence, enrolled them in his service, among the seventy-two. Luke names one of them, the most illustrious, or the one who was the source of his information (Lk 24:18).

Even if he does leave traces of some itineraries, our evangelist does not have the custom of giving the names of villages or the measure of distances: he amazes us here with his geographical precisions. Yet, he does not give them to show his erudition, but because they are essential to certain aspects of this singular story: neither the name of the village nor the distance from Jerusalem are indifferent elements. It was not the desire of Luke to inscribe in his gospel any but the apparitions at Jerusalem. He therefore names Emmaus here somewhat like he named Arimathea earlier, qualifying it as a town of the Jews (Lk 23:51); Emmaus was, for him, part of the distant outskirts of Jerusalem. Only, this village was not at the gate of the town, for, and this is another quite remarkable side of the adventure, Jesus walked a good bit of time with his two companions.

Luke wished to portray two things: on the one hand, Jesus showed himself to several, on the very day of his Resurrection, within the circle of the Holy City; on the other hand, he pushed his friendship even to the point of catching at the exit two of his disciples who were going back to their homes discouraged, and gave them along the road a course in Sacred Scripture. In the thought of the evangelist, then, these two concurrent circumstances were necessary: sufficient road that the Master have time to explain himself; yet not too much, so that the entire event might remain within the radius of the City and that the two disciples would even have time to be back there before nightfall.

In the transmission of the text there is some hesitation between sixty stadia and one hundred and sixty stadia. The considerations coming from the internal criticism which I have just exposed seem to me to be a reason to prefer the sixty stadia. The stadium being about two hundred yards, sixty of them would make a distance of around eight miles: this was in itself an appreciable trip, yet one which would not take a person outside of the suburbs, while one hundred and sixty stadia, more than twenty miles, would take one too far away. To be sure, twenty miles, six hours of walking, would have permitted more talk, but such a lengthy conversation was not necessary. Seven or eight miles, two hours on the road, this seems about right, especially if Jesus did his two disciples the favor of joining them at the gate of the town.

The two men had left the place in the afternoon. They were discouraged in the heavy mourning which had crushed them for three days, and abashed at all the stir which had arisen since morning in their little community. One would say that they had not even taken the trouble to go to the tomb. We see them on the road which would take them back to their village. The evangelist, who clearly specifies that Jesus himself approached to walk along with them, finds it cumbersome to explain to the reader that even so they did not recognize him: Their eyes were made powerless to recognize him, he writes. And how do you think he could speak without a certain mystery about so great a mystery?

Aside from this, everything is portrayed quite naturally, after the manner of a meeting and conversation which might spring up between men traveling on foot along a highway. The two disciples chat about the events which have so overwhelmed them: nothing could be more understandable. But that a pilgrim, coming out of Jerusalem, would be unaware of the great and sad affair and not be able to divine it at seeing both of them so dejected, this was beyond them! Was it possible that this stranger could be so ignorant of that which filled them so, or that he remained so indifferent to it?

They come to a halt in their journey, and assume a sad air, the text says; the word can also signify a sullen air. One of them expresses their astonishment. Perhaps they asked themselves if this ignorance might not be a pretence? Could this stranger be an enemy of Jesus? No, not at all; he had every appearance of being sincere; his question is posed guilelessly. The conversation proceeds by brief, stirring phrases, cut by pauses: it seems as though the two disciples are practically breathless. Nevertheless, their remarks, thus placed end to end, provide us with a precise and penetrating exposition of the situation, which confirms what we know or suspect from other sources. We have here an image of the occurrences and, what is still more precious, an image of souls, a tableau of the Church at the dawn of the Resurrection of the Lord.

Cleopas and his companion have the feeling of belonging to a community, which although still nameless was aware of existing: "Some women who were with us... several of ours...", they say in moving and simple fashion. Yet, they do not consider themselves as separated from the Jewish community; they say with respect: "Our ruling Priests and our leaders"; they do not break away from their nation, even when they express their sorrowing regret at what it had done.

They have the highest kind of idea of Jesus. Conversing with a stranger, met by chance on their trip, they do not bring to the surface the whole of their thought; what they say is the least that could be said, but in itself it is not lacking in grandeur: A renowned rabbi, mighty in words and in works, sacred to God and high in the esteem of men. They do not risk giving him the name of Christ, the discretion of their Master had left its mark on them; but they do suggest this name: "He who is to deliver Israel." These two men are above all penetrated with an extraordinary fervor with regard to Jesus: they think only of him, they speak of him alone; fifteen times on this page resounds the pronoun "him." As disabled as they might be, the two disciples are not undone; they are overflowing with tenderness and veneration.

According to them, a keen emotion reigned since the morning in the little community of Jesus Christ. Some women of this community asserted that they had seen angels who said to them: "He is alive." But the men did not believe them. This would have been too good on their part. And then, was it possible that the women could have been the first to know? Nonetheless, several had gone in the course of the morning to visit the tomb and had found it empty. Not only Peter and John whom the Magdalene had set in motion in the morning; but still others, whom the other women had set astir. Mary the mother of James, Salome the mother of the other James, did not allow their sons to languish "in mourning and in tears" (Mk 16:10); they must have urged them to take themselves to the sepulcher. Do you think that Joseph of Arimathea could have restrained himself from going to see what had happened at his own tomb, and that Nicodemus might have remained insensible to the sequence of his generous initiative? It would be unlikely that such disciples would not have run to see for themselves. They found everything as the women had said; unhappily, him, they did not see. Yet, this was the essential thing. If he had truly risen, why was he delaying in showing himself? What did he need to have said, and then, by women?

Our two men appear to have been confused by this: one would say that it was because of this that they did not become a part of all the commotion. Basically, the idea that their Master might have risen was not so foreign to these two disciples: the evocation of the "third day" is a recollection of the predictions of Jesus, they are disturbed and unhappy to feel this third day slip away. They might have, in this case, waited for the end of it before taking to the road: logic would demand this. But what is the use of seeking logic in bruised hearts, in souls in disarray?

If these two disciples were not men "noble and good of heart" (Lk 8:15), would Jesus have granted them the grace of joining them as he did, and of delivering to them so beautiful an instruction? By the fashion in which he takes them on, he very soon appeared to them to be a man of eminence, not much involved in the events of the day, but quite versed in the Sacred Letters, and on a very high plane in his meditation upon the divine plans. He offers them, as they walk, an entire course on Messianism. He takes the Bible from the beginning, from Moses, and he continues through the Prophets; he traverses its highlights in order to extract the profound thought: the Messiah must through suffering attain to glory, the great men who had preceded him had known this fate and had followed this way, and great annunciations also pointed in this direction.

How little open you are to the Scriptures and to the prophetic announcements. You ought to understand, the traveler says, that the misfortune which has come upon the great man in whom you have put your trust is not a proof that he was not the Christ, but could well be on the contrary the best proof that veritably he is the Messiah! The stranger said this in a warm and persuasive voice; he put all of his soul into it: this must have been a holy rabbi, on the perimeter of the official circles. He made such a profound impression on the two disciples that they were ashamed to ask him his name. They are far from the rather free and easy reflection which had been theirs at the initial moment of the encounter.

We see them now at the end of the journey. The rabbi seems to be about to continue on his way. Then, with extreme insistence, even to the point of doing him respectful violence, they implore him to consent to spending the night with them. The late afternoon hours approached, and for Orientals this already constituted the end of the day: such was the pretext given by the two disciples. The truth was that they could not resolve themselves to leaving their astonishing companion when they were so near to their homes, along the edge of the highway, and thus see him continue his way all alone. They think of all the honor he would do their village if he would agree to accept their hospitality; if they were so insistent, it was not in order to have him stay in the inn, but to have him dwell with them. And, quite proud of his acceptance, they in fact receive him with all due respect.

What could be more moving than this posthumous visit of Jesus in a little village in the environs of Jerusalem! He must do once more, in the most simple way in the world, what he did in his first life. The inhabitants salute him: he is affable toward all, attentive to the humble people, endearing toward the children.

While the women prepare the supper and the table, the men do him the honors of the houses and fields. He is not insensitive to these good things of the earth, because to leave them had always been presented by him as a sacrifice, and to find them again, a reward (Mk 10:29-30 and parallels). This Risen One, who was therefore no longer of the earth, nevertheless walked the land and tramped the streets of Emmaus.

Although he was so perfectly identical to himself, no one among the villagers recognized him. He had that agility which allowed him to mold his demeanor according to the pleasure of his spirit, so that he would be known only when he willed and as he willed. When the time came, the unknown guest presided over the meal. He accomplished the usual actions of the master of the household, pronounced the blessing, effected the breaking of the bread, and took care of the distribution, acts which were sacred to the Israelites, especially in the hands of a rabbi. Jesus fulfilled them with the great religious quality that was his: by this his disciples recognized him.

Their eyes were opened, it was all so plain: it was he whom they saw. But, no sooner was he recognized than, behold, he had disappeared, before they could touch him, before he had started to eat. At other meetings he will condescend to all this; this time, no. And indeed, through this contact with Jesus, Cleopas and his comrade had been favored beyond all expectation. If the sensible contact had not been prolonged as they would have liked, still they were blessed with a spiritual contact of which they would never even have dreamed; and the latter was more precious than anything. They become aware of this and between them they enter into reflection: the long conversation along the road could only have its source in Jesus; no one except him could speak in this way, only he could thus unveil the Scriptures. Immediately they left their little village and got back to the Holy City in order to testify that they had seen Jesus and that he was indeed living. They urgently desired to render this testimony, to him who had done such a favor for them, and to their brothers who were still in mourning.

The blessing and breaking of the bread were not a renewal of the Eucharist: Jesus did nothing which any rabbi would not have done. Luke, in recounting the matter, is not thinking of the Lord's Supper. Moreover, he will say in a moment that Jesus along with the Eleven and their companions take only a most ordinary nourishment, a bit of grilled fish (Lk 24:41-42). Yet there is a crescendo from one manifestation to the next: before the two disciples Jesus disappeared without eating, before the Eleven he consents to eat. Luke does not truly seem to wish to say that Jesus honored with his Eucharist the two from Emmaus.

On the other hand, Luke emphasizes a great deal the importance of the profound instruction given along the road to Emmaus, namely: that what had happened to the Lord, the victory over death, the glory through ignominy, had been foretold and prefigured by the Prophets. This thought which will so greatly occupy the primitive Church as the first discourses of Peter verify, is referred to Jesus himself. He took the trouble, Luke writes, to decipher Scripture, to single out its profound orientations, and to show how they converged toward him, particularly toward his Passion and his Resurrection. The two disciples had not kept to themselves the lesson of Sacred Scripture which they had been the first to savor. We can suppose that Jesus had the goodness to repeat it for others and that this was one of the subjects treated in the conversations throughout the forty days.

The discourse along the route allowed Jesus to refine the spirit of his disciples, and to prepare them to believe. That they did not see him until they already believed, that through possessing faith they arrived at vision, is this not the indication that their faith created the vision, and that the latter was nothing but a kind of religious hallucination? Not at all. The vision is presented in the firm conditions of human experience. But Jesus willed that those who saw him stop not at the Man, but learn how to reach even to God. He willed that they give their adhesion to that which constituted, in what they saw, the object itself of faith. Now the object of faith, we must never forget, is always a mystery of God, known through the words of God, and believed upon these very words.

Furthermore, among those who will be in possession of the true faith, Jesus seeks only good subjects, docile and understanding. It was not his desire to extort their adhesion, but that it surge up "from the heart": he says so, and in his tongue the heart is the spirit. Hence the concern to dispose the disciples to experience the fact of his Resurrection and to lead them to believe in the mystery invested in this fact. The whole of this preparation deserves admiration: it implies not only homage to the divine majesty, but respect for the human heart; the four gospels vouch for this.

If the two disciples from Emmaus merited the reproach of not having much clear-sightedness and of having "a heart" slow to believe, it is because they resisted the invitations, the explanations, which ought to have conducted them to belief. They had not even given themselves, although their hearts were all afire at that particular moment, when Jesus in person, walking side by side with them, gave them their lesson; they did not believe until after having seen. The remainder of the disciples did no better: they did not believe until after having seen; they even refused to lend faith to the testimony of the men or the women who had seen Jesus before them.

This story of the disciples from Emmaus seemed so typical to the author who concluded the gospel of Mark that he had, in his curtailed ending, the happy inspiration of retracing it in abridged form. "Following upon this," he writes (he means the apparition to Magdalene), "he appeared, in another form, to two of the disciples: he appeared to them as they were journeying and going into the countryside; the latter also came back to announce this to the others, but they had no more faith in them" (that is: than they had had in Mary Magdalene) (Mk 16:12-13).

In these other disciples there is no need to see merely the Apostolic College, for the author assigns to the latter, immediately afterwards, a special place and treatment, in reverently calling them the Eleven (Mk 16:14). There ought to be understood here either simple disciples without any particular designation, or disciples of the category of the seventy-two. On the whole, they had been slow to believe; neither the word of the Prophets and of Jesus himself, nor the testimony of the women or men who had been the first to see him had sufficed to form their faith in the Resurrection of Jesus.

CHAPTER 5

THE APOSTLES SEE JESUS

Ten Apostles and Some Disciples See Jesus

This final word about the rather general "incredulity" persisting among the disciples does not in any way contradict what follows in the reading of Luke. According to him, the two disciples return in haste to Jerusalem. They are burning to bring in their testimony and to reassure their brothers. They meet some who are still sad and gloomy as they themselves were, and who do not believe them. Nevertheless, they have the good fortune to find the Eleven and others with them in a better frame of mind. Let us read what Luke has to say.

> They [the two from Emmaus] having thus arisen right away, returned to Jerusalem. They found gathered together [the word means: crowded, pressed against one another, numerous] the Eleven and those who were with them. They were in the process of saying this: "The Lord has really risen, and he has been seen by Simon." Then, in their turn, they recounted what had happened to them along the road, and how they had recognized him in the breaking of the bread. And as they were conversing in this manner, behold, there he was in the midst of them. "Peace be with you," he said to them. But, as they were completely dumbfounded and seized with fear, it seemed to them they were looking upon a ghost. And he said to them: "Why are you so troubled? And why do these uncertitudes arise in your hearts? See my hands and my feet. Take notice that it is

indeed I. Feel me and consider that a ghost has neither flesh nor bones as you see that I have." And, in saying this, he showed them his hands and his feet. But as they continued to be unbelieving, out of joy, and they did not come forth from their wonderment, he said to them: "Have you something here to eat?" They had nothing to offer him but a bit of grilled fish. Well then! He took what they offered him and he ate in their presence (Lk 24:33-43).

The two from Emmaus sought to reunite with not just any members of their community, but with the leaders, Peter, the Eleven. They had the good fortune to find them meeting together. Luke does not say where. John, recounting the same meeting, does not say where either. Some think of the Cenacle. Yet nothing demands that it be there. Some see, rather, a more spacious house, less fancy. The Eleven and those who were with them were squeezed against each other, as if in the diminutive room of a modest dwelling. The provision of food in the house was scanty: when Jesus asked if there was something to eat, they had only a bit of fish to present to him. Since everything inclines us to believe that the meeting had been summoned by Peter, it must have taken place where he was staying.

The two pilgrims from Emmaus found the assembly in dispositions which they had not expected. Not only did they not have any trouble in having their testimony accepted; but an unimpeachable testimony had preceded theirs. An event of the first order had come to pass: Simon Peter had seen Jesus. He had assembled his brothers to let them know about it; this is why they were there, the Ten along with Peter, and others with them, all on the way to believing in the Resurrection upon the word of him to whom Jesus had said: "You, when you have come back, strengthen your brothers in the faith" (Lk 22:32). Peter tells how he had seen Jesus. Not one of the evangelists relates to us the details or the circumstances of the meeting. It becomes the major occurrence of the day, after that of the Resurrection itself.

The word of Peter counts more than anything. It is he who brings his colleagues to believe and prepares them for the vision. All of these men conferring among themselves come to be convinced that doubt is no longer possible: "Really, they say, the Lord has risen since he has been seen by Simon!" The two from Emmaus add their experience to that of their chief, and their testimony to his. Faith spreads through the assembly; it grows within the spirit. John, taking up the account of this meeting again, will tell us: Nonetheless, someone among the Eleven showed himself resistant and departed.

As for Peter himself, he too had to believe before seeing; several hints on the part of John have helped us to get an idea of this initial faith of Simon Peter. He told himself that, the might of God having been exercised on the corpse of Jesus, his Master had risen from the dead and ascended to heaven, and perhaps would not be seen again. Not knowing very well what attitude to adopt before his brothers, what directive to give them, or whether to rejoice or to continue to weep, Peter shut himself up in solitude and prayer. He thus remained a good part of the day, until noon, until afternoon, until the blessed moment when his beloved Lord came suddenly to set himself before him, demonstrating that he was risen, confirming that He desired to precede them and group them together again in Galilee. Peter henceforth was secure; he recovered his tranquil assurance, he resumed his role as leader. It was then that he convoked his brothers. Messengers had run throughout the town to find all of them.

Their conference was drawn out through the evening. Such was the first council of the Church, that in which was affirmed the faith in the Resurrection of Jesus. At twilight, in the brightness of the lamps, these men were content to once more find themselves about Peter. With him they were safe; and this was the first time they had seen each other since the great drama which had scattered them. They felt themselves reviving. What Peter told them reanimated in them their hope at the same time as their faith. He too was happy to testify on behalf of his Master, to execute the orders received from him and to rekindle the flame in the hearts of his brothers.

This, then, is the tableau. Squatted in the same room, conversing freely, mingling with one another fraternally, there they were when, behold, all at once Jesus was in the midst of them! We must put ourselves in their place, imagine all of the circumstances, if we wish to grasp in its full relief the truth of the account of Luke. The evangelist has retained above all the impression of amazement and also of fear which had taken hold of those in assistance. Ah! perhaps not all, perhaps neither Peter nor those who had already seen Jesus; and yet, he appeared with such suddenness, and endowed with such inconceivable subtlety, with so surprising an agility, he stood there in all of his radiance with such great vigor, freshness and beauty, that, even when one had already seen him, he was completely startled to see him again. We are not astonished that the disciples were greatly disturbed.

No one knows how he entered. He hailed them familiarly. He moved, he spoke, he enveloped all of them with his glance, he once more took his place in the midst of them in the simplest way in the world. Their eyes were riveted to him with fervor and with stupor, but they were so little accustomed to such a sight that it seemed to them they were looking upon a ghost. Then came about the scene of more or less experimental verification, so natural to behold, and recounted by Luke with such great tact, in which Jesus endeavors to give palpable proof of the reality of his body and of the perfect identicalness of Person. Amiably, he asks his disciples to touch him: this was not difficult for them, so close was he to them. He presented to them his hands, not only in order that they might take them, but so that they might explore the scars of his martyrdom; and this is why he said: Look at my hands and also at my feet, while slipping through their ranks so that all might look and make their verification.

A profound joy began to well up in the hearts of these men, the very joy which he himself had announced to them and which no one would be capable of taking from them (Jn 16:22). They felt their heavy sadness shattered and turned into this wonderful joy (Jn 16:20). So overwhelming was the spectacle that they could not believe their eyes. As they did not come out of their astonishment, and he wished to bring them back to a more ordinary level, he pushed his condescension still further. Having had them look through the house for some leftover food, he began to nibble on a bit of grilled fish, their customary lunch. They were quite aware that it was not out of hunger he was eating: in his glorious body, the vegetative or animal life, the physical and chemical aspects of the organs were completely subordinate to the will of the spirit. If it was his pleasure to eat in the presence of these men, it was by way of a kind of a fantasy to which he lent himself, in order to demonstrate to them through the most familiar of human activities the truth of a perfectly human resurrection. The disciples were down-to-earth individuals, as peasants and herdsmen can be. Jesus offered them the favor of these material demonstrations: they increased their conviction and took nothing from his glory, they offered to them peace of heart and light for their spirit.

Everything happens at the end of Luke's gospel as if, from the day of the Resurrection, Jesus imprinted on Christian thought a definitive orientation and brought to achievement the revelation of the divine plan. Luke completely leaves aside the meetings in Galilee. They were not unknown to him; but they did not fit into his work. More than Matthew, more than Mark, and long before John, Luke made it known that Galilee had not absorbed the public life of Jesus; Judea had also had its part. Jerusalem holds an eminent place in this gospel: Jesus travels with mystery toward the Holy City, he enters there with emotion. It is in Jerusalem that he must consummate his sacrifice and show himself in his Resurrection; it is from there that he is to go back to heaven and that those who are his must set out to propagate over the earth the Church and the Gospel.

Luke will finish his first work and begin his second, the book of the Acts, with this magnificent vision. This, then, is why he has concentrated the entire gospel of the Ascension around the Holy City. To recount the apparitions in Galilee would have deformed this excellently presented abridgement. All of the

events seem to belong to the same day, even though the curtailed character of the account is unmistakable. And furthermore,
at the debut of the Acts, Luke informs us that Jesus for forty days
appeared to the apostles and spoke to them of the Reign of God
(Ac 1:3).

Luke is, therefore, as original in the way he terminates his
gospel as he was in the part which is proper to him, precisely the
account of the journey in the direction of Jerusalem. He no longer
has anything in common either with Matthew or with John in
what they themselves have of a distinctive nature; as for his usual
conformity with Mark, it necessarily had to cease to exist. For
the ensemble as well as for the details of the account of the Resurrection, Luke is completely personal.

The evangelists no more report all the instructions they
received than they relate all the manifestations of Jesus. Of the
lessons given by the Christ in the course of these forty days, each
reports according to the pleasure of his inspiration those which
seem to him to be the most important. We can, therefore, post-
pone until later and collect together these extremely significant
teachings of Jesus such as they have been handed down through
the different writers, so that we might better understand them.
For the time being, we continue to pursue the occurrences. We
are presently at the manifestation of Sunday evening when Jesus
showed himself to the Eleven and to other disciples assembled
in Jerusalem. John resumes the account of this apparition, he
adds several features to it, he makes the sequence to it known.
This renewed treatment and addition are of the sharpest interest; they help us look deeper into what occurred and allow us to
divine the complexity of the events.

Thomas Sees Jesus

The last evangelist marks in his own discreet way the
abridged aspect of the accounts of his predecessors. Between the
composition of Matthew which is completely orientated toward

Galilee and that of Luke which totally concentrates upon Jerusalem, he slips his own, into which he introduces certain facts which came to pass at Jerusalem and others which took place in Galilee: he thus in a sense confirms each of his predecessors. He is careful not to omit the apparitions in the City itself of the martyrdom; he knew that it was they which, after the three days of sadness and of uncertitude, had convinced and reassured the principal disciples before Jesus met with them again in Galilee. Yet, one of the Eleven had resisted and did not come back until the end of eight days: John tells of this also.

First of all, John did not wish that anyone think the embalming on Friday evening had been badly carried out: the men who had taken charge of this had performed their task well; "the manner in use among the Jews" did not demand greater refinement (Jn 19:40). And, when he recounts the embassy of the women on Sunday morning, John does not speak at all of their spiced ointments, nor of their desire to add the quality of the perfumes they had bought to the large quantity of myrrh and aloes procured by Nicodemus.

Moreover, the only woman involved in action in this gospel is Magdalene. Having come at a very early hour to the tomb (Jn 20:1), and seeing it open, she ran to alert Peter and the other disciple, who was John himself; and each of them was set on the path to belief (Jn 20:10). Magdalene next is the first to see the Risen Christ and the first to announce the Resurrection. She informed the disciples that Jesus was indeed the same and was quite willing to be touched, but nevertheless would not allow that she tarry with him, because his renewal of his life in their midst was in itself the beginning of his Ascension (Jn 20:18).

All of these initial facts concerned with the Resurrection of the Lord are assigned to the "first day of the week." This day, carefully noted at the start of the account and repeated at the debut of the passage where we now find ourselves, gives a solemn air to the narration. The second time, the demonstrative adjective "this particular day, this well known day," intimates that such a day had become among the Christians, and well merited to do so, the first of the week, and veritably the first of days (Jn 20:1, 19). On the interior of this incomparable day, another particularity, the account transports us from the morning to the evening, as if nothing happened between the two. John seems to underline that the disciples had remained throughout this day, the third after the death of Jesus, in great expectation.

> It was therefore evening, on this particular day, the first of the week; and, in the place where the disciples were, the doors were firmly shut, because of the fear which they had of the Jews, when Jesus came and stood in their midst. "Peace to you!" he declared to them. Then, when he had said this, he showed them his hands and his side. Of course, the disciples were overjoyed to see the Lord. He said to them once more, then: "Peace be with you! . . . As the Father has sent me, I also send you." Then, when he had said this, he breathed upon them: "Receive the Holy Spirit," he declared to them, "those whose sins you pardon, they will be pardoned them; those from whom you withhold pardon, pardon will be withheld from them."
> Thomas however, one of the Twelve, the one called Didymus, was no longer with them when Jesus came. Naturally, the other disciples said to him: "We have seen the Lord." But he replied to them: "If l do not see in his hands the imprint of the nails, and if I do not put my hand into his side, I shall not believe." Again, eight days later, his disciples were once more inside, and Thomas was with them: Jesus came, the doors were tightly shut. Then he stood in the midst of them and said to them: "Peace to you!" Next, he declared to Thomas: "Bring your finger here and carefully inspect my hands; and bring your hand also and put it into my side; and then, be not incredulous, but believing." In response, Thomas said to him: "My Lord! My God!" Jesus said to him: "Because you have seen, behold, you have believed! Blessed are those who have not seen and yet have believed!" (Jn 20:19-29).

John here applies his own method which consists in retaining one example characteristic of a situation. He goes back to the first apparition to the principal disciples, recounted by Luke (Lk 24:36-43). To the traits so well portrayed by his predecessor, he adds certain recollections full of interest for us. He points out the clandestine and timorous character of the assembly: these men, of whom the majority were Galilean, lived in fear of the Jewish rulers, all of the doors of the house were closed off. Yet we see Jesus in the midst of them, by the subtlety of his risen body and by an unprecedented gift of penetration.

John emphasizes next, not, as Luke has done, the reaction of surprise, but the extreme familiarity of the scene: the current formula of salutation, only with a more stirring intonation on account of having to make the offering of peace after such a rude shock; the presentation of his hands, of his incomparable hands rendered more venerable by the scars of the crucifixion; the showing of his side pierced by the lance. Jesus could have made this demonstration only in a beautiful gesture of friendship: he is seen to undo with a natural motion the clothing or the appearance of clothing, with which he honorably adorned his risen body. In himself recounting so simply these details, the evangelist who had been the witness of them surrounds with great human charm the posthumous glory of Jesus. And concerning this matter, we are not at the end of our marveling as the fourth gospel draws to a close.

The manifestation recounted here by John is the only one which he reports as taking place on the behalf of the apostles. He connects thereto the conferral of the great powers which were in fact accorded to the apostolic hierarchy in the course of the forty days and which were of the greatest interest for the constitution of the new Reign. But, as regards the moment at which took place this complement to ordination, there is no need to take things too literally. The text itself makes it apparent enough that in the thought of the evangelist the words of Jesus are inscribed at this spot parenthetically: we shall unite them to others of the same kind. Several of the manifestations of Jesus before his death were ordinations: he will do the same after death.

Here it is to Thomas that John desires to come. The first evangelists had not designated anyone by name; the final evangelist did not see anything inexpedient in Thomas' being named as the type of those who had resisted the light of faith. Neither the evidence of the empty tomb, nor the consideration of the Scriptures, nor reflection on the words of Jesus had stirred this apostle. Nor did he surrender himself to the testimony of his brothers, not even to that of Peter. Either he did not come to the meeting called by Peter; or he came, but did not remain until the end; he was not there, or he was no longer there, the evangelist tells us, when Jesus arrived.

It is from this point on that he aggravates his position and hardens himself in his incredulity: to the precise and warm affirmations of his brothers he opposed a doubling of demands and of denials; such a disposition of spirit was just too much. None of these Galileans had shown himself very inclined to believe; but Thomas went beyond all bounds. They presented him with a detailed account of what they had seen. I wish to see more closely, he replied to them; and indeed, he added, seeing is not sufficient, he must be touched if it is really he. Thomas insisted upon verifying the identity of the crucified, by putting his finger in the scars left by the nails and his whole hand in the wound in the side.

Jesus will lend himself with admirable condescension to all the demands of his disciple, but after having left him for eight days in his incredulity. John is insistent about this delay; on the other hand, he describes with such brilliance the act of faith of his unbelieving brother that it becomes quite plain that during this time a very special grace had been working on this crude youth. Thomas also loved his Master; only he was quite down-to-earth and obstinate, he wanted proofs to his own liking.

Therefore, the paschal feasting being finished, the Lord having doubtlessly again shown himself during the week and thus confirmed the rendezvous in Galilee, the disciples were once more assembled in a meeting with Peter. They do not seem to have been in a hurry to depart, now that they had seen Jesus and their joy was so profound. They had assembled in order to pray in common, to thank the Lord God for what he had done for the sake of his Son Jesus, and to prepare themselves for setting out on the journey together. Thomas was there, of course: the idea of separating from his brothers had not entered his mind.

Now, we see Jesus again in their midst, as if to approve the departure and to direct the caravan. But, first, he has to deal with the unbeliever. The scene was close to every memory. Did Jesus in effect place his two hands beneath the two eyes of the apostle? Did he in fact take hold of his finger and his hand to place them in his wounds? The text seems to say so. However, the profession of faith is so spontaneous, it appears to have been so prompt, that there is reason to think that Thomas surrendered himself at first sight without demanding anything more. He is plainly inspired, he is beneath the blow of grace, his expression is splendid, his faith goes to the limit. In the Man, he recognizes the God. He is the first to say this, he who was the last to give himself. No one yet, in the Gospel, had unequivocally awarded this name of "God" to Jesus. Such a profession would have been too far beyond the Israelites: Thomas was the first to master this transcendence, in the light of the risen Christ.

John certainly wishes to suggest that the beauty of this declaration of faith compensated to a very high degree for the excessive incredulity. Nevertheless, Jesus offered a reproach, through an interrogative phrase, which was tempered by a friendly smile: Well, you are here this time? And now you have had a sufficient view of me, for you believe so well? Even in this reproach Jesus pays homage to the perfected faith of the disciple. But he does not fail to pay homage also to the faith of others, who had the merit of believing before having seen. The entire gospel of the Resurrection shows appreciation for this merit.

The author of the closing verses of Mark also very probably refers to this apparition in the presence of Thomas when after having recalled that Jesus appeared first of all to Mary of Magdala and next to the two disciples from Emmaus, he writes:

"Finally he appeared last of all to the Eleven, while they were at table; he reproached them for their incredulity and the hardness of their heart, because they had not even believed those who had plainly seen him in his risen state" (Mk 16:14).

This apparition reported without the least indication of time or of place is like a lightly sketched tableau. The author would appear to say that the lack of belief and the hardness of heart were characteristic of several of the disciples. This was in fact probably the case, since John is not afraid to say that this was met with even in the case of one of the Twelve. Around the mystery of the Man-God, these Twelve had been the field of the greatest of religious experiences. These things had given them a great deal upon which to reflect. It was inevitable that upon contact with the Christ "the thoughts of the heart" be revealed, the most profound traits which a man carried within himself in relation to God (Lk 2:35).

This schema suffices to characterize the manner in which the disciples had come to the faith. What follows equally recapitulates the mission which Jesus had given them, that of propagating this faith; this author also reproduces a specimen of the words uttered by Jesus. As nothing obliges us here either to attach them to the scene which precedes them and seems to command them, we shall arrange them alongside those which are drawn from the other evangelists.

The Quality of the Facts and the Witnesses

Before leaving the theater of the first manifestations, let us remark the modality in which they were vested. Jesus treated his disciples, and very particularly the Eleven, as free men. He did not take them by enthusiasm, he did not trust himself to sensitivity or to sentiment, he revealed himself to them through the light of intelligence and through all the rays of the spirit. They had to understand that "He had risen as he had said he would." He enabled them to have, with regard to his Resurrection from among the dead, the most astounding experience which man might have, that which would be of the most interest to the future of mankind in time and in eternity. It was necessary that this experience, which they will exclusively have the privilege of enjoying, unveil to them its full content; this is why he willed that their spirit be sufficiently open to grasp that it came from God and that it conducted to God: "I ascend to my Father and your Father, my God and your God."

There was no need for them to come under the reproach which on an earlier occasion he had addressed to the Jews: "You are greatly in error" (Mk 12:27), it is not in your spirit that the Scriptures could be the Word of God, or that the Resurrection might be within the Power of God (Mk 12:24 and parallels). And Jesus did not manifest himself to his disciples until they had this understanding, and were willing to offer themselves to this grace.

In this is the profound response to the objection constantly reasserted: Why did he not show himself to those who had condemned him? Why did he not present himself in a session of the Sanhedrin, as he did in the midst of his friends? There is no trace of this objection having come to the minds of the disciples. They no doubt comprehended that, if the Lord had granted this favor to his enemies, they would only have plunged themselves deeper into their incredulity, or it would have extorted from them an adhesion which would have amounted to nothing. Those who had put him to death were still too badly disposed against him. In the long run, perhaps, some of them would soften and be converted. But at that time, the members of the Sanhedrin could not qualify as witnesses to the Resurrection.

Furthermore, Jesus had forewarned them, and this is a point which we too often forget. He had pronounced majestically before them, at the hearing in which they had condemned him, a strange declaration which had made them jump. The three synoptics report it with slight variations which lead us to the following meaning, which is apparent enough in Matthew: "You will not see the Son of Man again except sitting at the Right of the Power and coming on the Clouds of Heaven" (Mt 26:64; Lk 22:69; Mk 14:62).

Rather than his ultimate Parousia, Jesus had in view his proximate Return and his immediate Enthronement "in his own Kingdom", that is, his Church. He would have his judges understand: You will be able to understand that it is I who am reigning; but you will not see me again except in the sphere of God (for the Power here is God, and likewise the Clouds of Heaven). Jesus means to say to the members of the Sanhedrin: I shall not come to you again as a brother but as a God. Perhaps there was even in his word the threat of punishment which he had predicted at other times and he meant: You will feel my presence as one feels the Wrath of Yahveh. In any event, he wanted them to understand: You will no longer see me on this earth and you will hold me no more in your hands.

The Jews could not be witnesses. On the other hand, the disciples had to be. They said so incessantly: "This Jesus, God has raised him up; we are the witnesses" (Ac 2:32, 3:15). And sometimes they added: "We, and the Holy Spirit given by God to those who obey him" (Ac 5:32). They were conscious of being qualified witnesses. They explain themselves: "God has consecrated... Jesus of Nazareth... God was with him... God raised him up on the third day and enabled him to make himself seen, not to all of the people, but to the witnesses whom he himself had chosen in advance, to us who have eaten and drunk with him after his resurrection from among the dead" (Ac 10:38-41).

They alone could fully recognize him, with entire comprehension of the mystery. They alone could identify him with total security, they who had eaten and drunk with him, before as well as after, after as before. The others, who had not experienced his intimacy, the intimacy to which nothing could be compared and which nothing could replace, might have been doubtful about his identity. They could always have conjectured: Is this in fact he? What is he doing here? What does he want with us? For the true disciples, on the contrary, everything that derived from him became certitude and a sign of recovery. They recognized him in his most familiar attitudes, in his customary gestures, by the way he carried his head, by the expressions on his face, the ring of his voice, his way of giving the greeting of peace and of breaking bread, his fashion of calling them by their names as his friends.

Above all, they would find him again in his teaching. He repeated the same things to them as before; he staidly resumed the same conversations, especially those of the hours of intimacy. This is why so many of the passages which John has placed at the end of the Lord's Supper would be just as well in place after the Resurrection. Jesus engaged in the same discourses as if death had hardly interrupted them and had only rendered their accent more penetrating, their objects more intelligible.

These accumulated experiences manage to situate the mystery of Jesus in the regard of the disciples. They restore to them a Christ incontestably corporal and nevertheless possessing a marvelous mastery over the matter of our universe. He is revealed to them as completely spiritualized, endowed with a species of immensity and of ubiquity, agile with respect to everything, present to everything and seeing everything. No one went to him to let him know about the critical demands of Thomas; yet, he knew all of them, he had read even the most intimate thoughts of his disciple, he had labored on his heart.

"On that day," he had said to them, "you will no longer question me about anything... ; the hour is coming when I shall no longer speak to you in enigmas, but when I shall openly converse with you about the Father" (Jn 16:23, 25). It had come, this hour in which the disciples understood, in the words of their Lord and in the conditions of his new life, to what an extent his sacred Humanity was the personal possession of the Son of God and the perfect organ of the Divinity: "Philip, he who has seen me, has seen the Father; I am in the Father, and the Father is in me" (Jn 14:9, 10, 11).

MANIFESTATIONS IN GALILEE

Intimate Exchanges in Galilee

It was above all in Galilee that Jesus manifested himself. Throughout the forty days during which his Ascension was extended, the disciples must have spent about thirty in this province where the Lord had said he would meet them. He was no longer "localized" or limited to presence in any district, our conditions of existence no longer constrained him, he was no longer an inhabitant of the earth. He simply wished to remain in a way at the disposal of his own, in order to clearly demonstrate to them in the course of several weeks and by many proofs that he was truly living (Ac 1:3).

Almost all of them had originated from Galilee; it was there that they had tasted in his presence the longest and most decisive hours of friendship; it was natural that he invite them to find them once more in these environs. Moreover, a greater number of them could gather in that region with less risk; the disciples who might have come from Jerusalem and from Judea would be more at ease in Galilee then in their homes. Between the two feasts, that of the Pasch and that of Pentecost, which commemorated the great events of their sacred history, these Israelites will come to know the "palingenesis" of Jesus Christ (Mt 19:28). The first fruits of the new Church, they will taste of this renewal, flourishing throughout their lands and much more in their spirits, the rebirth which will be the first springtime of the Christian era.

75

We would love to know the details of these beautiful days; and we deplore, here more than elsewhere, the fragmentary nature and the gaps of our gospels. The Lord, in inspiring these writers, who were quite different from one another, did not desire that any of them further enlarge upon this subject. There is no need for our curiosity to stray beyond the essential: such is the thought that is here expressed in the last gospel. "It is indeed certain," it is written, "that Jesus performed before the eyes of the disciples a great quantity of other signs which will not be found consigned in this book; but these have been handed on so that you might believe that Jesus is the Christ, the Son of God, and so that, in this faith, you might have life through his name" (Jn 20:30-31).

This reflection could have flowed from the pen of John as the conclusion itself to the entire document. It certainly is concerned with the whole gospel, but most particularly with the gospel of the Resurrection. Thus the very object of the new faith is that Jesus is the Christ, the Messiah, that there is no other to await, and that this blessed Christ is veritably the Son of God, in the strict sense which he himself had always used and which John had always written. The evangelist did not write uniquely to give birth to this faith in the hearts of those who did not yet have it; it was his wish that his work contribute to its growth in those who already had it. He who possessed this great faith in the Christ possessed the incomparable life given in the Christ.

We come, then, with the disciples into this Galilee where the Lord had summoned them and had scarcely preceded them. Mark and Matthew have reported this convocation and accord to the rendezvous a good deal of importance. However, concerning the account of what happened, we have nothing to expect from Mark, since his gospel stops short. Matthew himself is content with an extremely summary tableau. Yet, throughout his gospel he has lent considerable importance to Galilee; he has reduced to a minimum the preaching in Judea and at Jerusalem, as well as the manifestation of Jesus in the Holy City after his

Resurrection: we could expect that he would be less reserved about the manifestation in Galilee. Luke gives us nothing about this chapter: we have said why.

As for John, even though he does not report the convocation, it is he who paints the most detailed tableau of the encounters. Following his usual method, he chooses one of them that is particularly significant; if the narration does not denote a literary adeptness, it does have a wonderful freshness about it. Everything leads us to believe that it is a question of the first meeting in Galilee to which Jesus had brought back his disciples. Perhaps because of this John chose this apparition in preference to others; in any case, a number of aspects could be better explained in this way.

"After this," John writes (that is, after the first manifestations in Jerusalem), "Jesus manifested himself another time to the disciples; this was at the sea of Tiberias."

The adverb which I translate by "another time" could signify simply "the next time" according to the bent of the text itself and the indication then slipped into the middle of the account where it is written: "Such was already the third manifestation by which Jesus made the disciples see that he was indeed risen from the dead" (Jn 21:14).

There is question, in this series, only of certain revelations to the disciples, and more particularly to the group which John continues to call the Twelve, even though now they are but the Eleven (Jn 20:19, 24, 26). The apparition to Magdalene, therefore, at present is not considered at all; and, calculating in this way, the manifestation on the shore of the sea of Tiberias is indeed, in the gospel of John, the third on behalf of the disciples. At the inception of the account, "the sea of Tiberias" is designated with emphasis by that name which must have been given to it more and more at the time when John was writing, because of the importance which had been assumed by the town of Tiberias since the ruin of Jerusalem. The image of this great sheet of water glistened in the memory of John, as an evocation of his youth and of the most radiant memory which he had of this Christ of whom he was the preferred disciple and whom he himself had loved so much.

Meeting at the Sea of Tiberias

At the sea of Tiberias, the Lord manifested himself like this: There were at the same spot Simon Peter, along with Thomas who was called Didymus, and Nathanael, who was from Cana in Galilee, there were also the two sons of Zebedee, as well as two others from among the disciples of Jesus. "I am going out to fish," Simon Peter said to them. "We also shall go with you," they declared to him. They went forth and got into the barque; but that night they caught nothing.

Now, morning having come already, Jesus was standing on the shore. However, the disciples were not aware that it was Jesus. Jesus asked them therefore: "Young men, don't you have any freshly caught fish?" They answered him: "No." He said to them then: "Throw the net over the right side of the barque, and you will discover some." Thus they cast it. And they did not have the strength to draw it up again because of the abundance of fish. "It is the Lord," declared then to Peter that disciple whom Jesus loved. Simon Peter, of course, from the instant that he heard the word: "It is the Lord," at once fixed his outer clothing about his waist, for he had stripped down, and threw himself into the sea, while the other disciples drew alongside with the barque, as they dragged with them the net of fish: it is true that they were not a great distance from land, but all the same they were about two hundred cubits.

When, therefore, they had landed, having allowed their net to drag, they noticed a well-made hearth of embers, with some fish upon it and some bread. Jesus said to them: "Bring here some of the fish you have just caught." Simon Peter, then, got back into the barque and he drew the net to land; it was filled with one hundred and fifty-three large fish, and, even though there were so many, the net had not broken. "Come and have breakfast," Jesus said to them. Not one of the disciples, furthermore, dared to ask him: "Who are you?" They knew that it was the Lord. Jesus drew near, took the bread and gave it to them, and also the fish. Such, then and there, was the third time that Jesus had made the disciples see that he had indeed risen from the dead (Jn 21:1-14).

There is throughout this page an admirable transparency. The disciples had, then, come back to Galilee as "their Lord" had requested: a title eight times repeated in the account. While waiting for Jesus to manifest himself, each of them had gone to make a tour of the place where he had lived and to carry to his friends the good news. John seems to say that the Lord did not delay his manifestation a very long time. But it came about in circumstances which no one could have foreseen.

It is to Peter that Jesus returns, and the others only benefit by the favor because they find themselves with Simon Peter. This page of John's only enhances the role of Peter. There are several of them there; they had remained grouped around him and even had come to dwell with him. And these were not the least among the disciples. There was Thomas, who had just compensated through so great an act of faith for his slowness to believe, and who perhaps was unwilling during such days to be separated from Peter, in order to be more certain of sharing the experiences and the thought of his chief. There was Nathanael, whom John has singled out from the beginning of the gospel as particularly versed in the Messianic interpretation of the Law and the Prophets (Jn 1:45). There were also with Simon Peter the two sons of Zebedee: we are not surprised at this, knowing to what an extent these three men were united to each other and to their Lord.

Why does John here name in the first place and with honor Thomas and Nathanael, so that the sons of Zebedee must come after them? No doubt out of modesty for himself and for his brother; but very likely also out of deference for his two colleagues. They were the intellectuals of the group, those who had the most critical spirit, the most mental acumen; John would appear to say: it was a fortunate thing that they were there. We ask ourselves why he mentions, and in this place alone, that Nathanael was from Cana of Galilee; we would find it more natural for him to have done so the first time that he presented him (Jn 1:45). Possibly he desires to pay him the honor here of not even having returned to his own region but having stayed with Peter. The other two disciples pointed out at the end were not of the Twelve. At Capernaum no doubt, in the house which he possessed, Peter had generously given hospitality to these friends of Jesus, who were also his own friends.

They had reflected together, prayed in common. But it was also necessary to eat, the guests had to be fed, no one should be made uncomfortable. Finding himself surrounded by his fishing gear in his little fisherman's house, Simon Peter quite naturally returned to what had once been his work. Hence, his proposal, the exit from the house, the mounting of the barque, the night at sea, all of which are so simply recounted by John. He and his brother were familiar with this type of work; but Thomas and Nathanael were not sailors: a man from Cana would not be accustomed to the sea. Yet we see them embarking with Peter, and spending an entire night at sea for nothing.

At the break of day they return empty-handed. Someone was on the shore! John writes awkwardly: "It was Jesus, but they did not see that it was he." They did not see, not because there was insufficient light, but because their eyesight was not lucid enough. At the request which is launched toward them they divine a client, a lover of fresh fish, someone happy to encounter coming to shore these very alert young men who must have made a good catch. The extremely dry "no" of their response betrays their discomfort: fishermen, like hunters, are not willing to admit they have caught nothing. At the suggestion of the man on the bank, however, our men consent to try one more cast with their net. He might be familiar with the lake, they said to themselves; we can always keep trying. Success did not have to be awaited and the catch was immediately so abundant that already it was impossible for them to haul in the net: this was truly a miraculous catch, one which reminded them of another.

When Jesus had attached to himself in a definitive manner Simon and the sons of Zebedee, he performed in the same surroundings, perhaps in the very same spot, a miracle of the same type, on which occasion he said to them: "I shall make of you fishers of men." This initial catch has not been recorded by John, but it has been by Luke who often depends on John (Lk 5:1-11). Certainly neither John nor Peter, who were men of the sea, had forgotten the marvelous catch their net had brought them. John was the first to recall it in these circumstances, and suddenly he had the intuition that it was the Lord who was across from them.

If John was quick to remember and perceptive in his intuition, it was Peter who had the sense of decision and promptness of execution. To arrive more quickly at the rendezvous with the Lord, he threw himself into the sea and splashed hurriedly toward the beach, after having simply wrapped his outer tunic around his waist. When the text says that Peter was stripped down, we do not need to take the matter literally. Peter did not spend this April night on his boat completely unclothed, for the weather would still be quite cool; but doubtlessly he had about him only his coarse fishing clothing which it was easy for him to roll up and which he was not afraid of getting wet. John means to say that Peter, although he was scantily garbed, with nothing on but the habit of his trade, did not hesitate at all to leap in all his nakedness into the presence of the Lord.

A loyal heart, a faithful friend! He was wonderful to see, on the morning of the Resurrection, winded in his rush to ascend to the holy sepulcher. He is admirable, again this morning, beating the water with his two legs, to make the first meeting of the Lord in Galilee. The others finished by oar, with their net dragging behind, the hundred yards which remained. Peter had had the instinct that he ought to be the first to be at the command of his Master. His comrades also left everything and leaped to land.

Their surprise was great: not only did they fail to see around the Lord the least heavenly majesty; but he had contrived to multiply the attentions of the earth with all of the simplicity that had been his before death. There were there the bright embers of a fire which to all appearances he had maintained; and over the embers fish and bread were beginning to cook. "Give me some of your fish, then," he said to them; they are fresher than mine! He was so insistent that Peter, who directed everything, had to get back into the boat and do a bit more work. God, what a catch! Their trade demanded that they count the large fish; John recalled that there were one hundred and fifty-three of them, and not a sign of a rip.

The evangelist seems to see in this miraculous cast of the net a profound symbol which possibly to his way of thinking united with the parable of the net (Mt 13:47). John could have discerned here, with time and the aid of the Spirit, the image of the Kingdom of Jesus. The Lord captures in the net of his Church a great quantity of fish of all kinds, many of which are large. Does the figure 153 also have a symbolical meaning? This is possible, but not certain. The catch was made under the helm of Peter. And the net did not break, as abundant and as lively as was the take. If John was thinking of all this when writing his account, he does not breathe a word about it and sticks to the most sober of narrations, with as much simplicity as he would use in describing an ordinary catch.

Everything unfolds in a most human manner, like the meeting at daybreak of good friends of whom some have worked throughout the night. "Come and have breakfast, you must be hungry," Jesus amiably says to them, after they had counted the fish; and it was he who did the honors at the little meal which he had employed himself in preparing. The account does not intimate there was a multiplication of bread or of fish in the hands of the Lord; rather, John emphasizes the humbleness of the scene: such great familiarity had bewildered them. He writes this in an embarrassed phrase. Upon seeing their Lord at such tasks, they were indeed anxious to ask him: Is it really you? — But none of them dared to do so, because they knew that, all the same, it was actually he. A certitude possessed them.

He gave himself completely to all that he did for them. "This," John writes — that is, this whole phenomenal ensemble translated by a simple neuter pronoun, which is most expressive here — was a new demonstration for them of the veritable Resurrection of Jesus. The third of this type, the evangelist says precisely: two other times in fact Jesus had allowed himself to be touched by his disciples, they had even given him something to eat; but this time it is he who takes care of feeding them. His attentions of such an earthly nature, rather unexpected on the part of a person who had risen, helped to identify him: his great goodness, his delicate charity had not changed. After he had thus renewed their strength, he began to speak to them of matters of the greatest import. It was a question of consolidating the Rock upon which the Church was to be built; and of making understood to everyone and to Peter himself that he had not lost the least degree of his role as Chief. In Jerusalem, it was to him that the Lord had already first shown himself; it was to him in the first place that he appeared in Galilee where it was his pleasure to regroup all of them. Let us listen to the stirring sequence in John.

The Lord with Simon Peter

> When, therefore, they had had their breakfast, Jesus said to Simon Peter: "Simon, son of John, do you cherish me more than these others do?" He answered him: "Yes, Lord, you well know that I love you." Jesus declared to him: "Feed my lambs." He said to him a second time: "Simon, son of John, do you cherish me?" He answered him: "Yes, Lord, you well know that I love you." Jesus declared to him: "Lead my sheep." He said to him for the third time: "Simon, son of John, do you love me?" Peter was sad-

dened at the fact that for the third time Jesus had said to him: "Do you love me?" And he responded to him: "You know everything, you know very well that I love you." Jesus declared to him: "Feed my sheep. Amen, amen, I say to you, when you were younger, you girded yourself and you went where you wished; but when you have grown old, you will stretch forth your hands, and someone else will bind you and will lead you forcibly where you would not go." He said this to him in order to indicate to him through what kind of death he would glorify God. Then, after he had said this to him, he addressed him: "Follow me."

Peter, turning around, noticed that the disciple whom Jesus loved had come up behind them. This was the very same person who, during the supper, had leaned over on his breast and had said to him: "Lord, who is the one who betrays you?" Having noticed him, therefore, Peter said to Jesus: "Lord, and what about him?" Jesus answered him: "Even if it is my will that he remain until I return, what does it matter to you? You, follow me." The rumor, then, spread among the disciples that this disciple would not die. Yet, Jesus had not said to Peter: "He will not die"; but: "If I desire that he remain until I come, what does it matter to you?" (Jn 21:15-23).

Commentators see in this scene a rehabilitation of Peter; the word is not well chosen: Peter did not have to be rehabilitated, the Lord had not denied him. But doubtlessly he did need to be reconfirmed, in his own eyes, and also before his brothers; hence this dialogue bearing the imprint of a singular grandeur and of so tender a friendship. Almost all of the verbs are in the present, thus rendering a great deal of life to the scene and presence to the personages. There is nothing to say that the three interrogations rushed upon one another, that there were not intervals between them making them more impressive. The first assault could have come, for example, during the small repast, when Peter, overwhelmed with delight upon receiving the food which Jesus tendered to him, cast in the direction of his Lord glances gleaming with affection and with respect.

If the threefold provocation on the part of Jesus was a discreet reminder of the triple denial of Peter and the means of effacing everything, it ought not to have been abruptly done, but gently and subtly. And this is why I am of the opinion that the appeal to friendship was not repeated in stronger and stronger terms, as one is inclined to believe, but on the contrary following a bent full of fine attenuations rendering the invitation more poignant. The dialogue unfolds in a solemn manner, intended by Jesus, but in no way strained. Even in his Resurrection, Jesus retains a simple nobility, one which is almost playful; he remains the nobleman.

Two words here designate the act of loving. One is more lofty, and presupposes a more select love, the love called *dilectio*: I have translated it by the verb "cherish," which, in this case and between men, takes on a nuance still more rare of distinction and of beauty. The other was more of a current term and more common in its meaning: it is quite simply the verb "to love."

Now, Peter answers with the more humble word, he does not dare to utter the more refined word, although it could have been in his thought that the latter would not be too strong to express the quality of his love. From the time of his denial, Peter had become mistrustful of himself. Yet he did not wish to belie his heart; he contented himself with offering it to Jesus and uncovering it before him who read it to its very depths.

But Jesus himself, when he questioned Peter, began with the more elevated term and finished with that which was more common. At first he said: "Do you cherish me more than your companions do?" Then, more simply: "Do you cherish me?" Finally, still more modestly: "Do you love me?" Peter is saddened at the fact that the quality of his love thus seems to be put in doubt. If Jesus solicits this love only in terms of declining intensity, this is on his part a friendly stratagem, one of those games in which a person indulges himself when he is loved a great deal and wishes to be told so, or to have himself told so. But Peter is so moved that he does not understand the matter so simply; he is sad on account of this persistence, as he was saddened when Jesus fixed his gaze upon him after the denial (Lk 22:61-62). Less desolate this time, he makes an appeal to this very scrutinizing gaze, he takes refuge in it in all security.

It was at this moment that Jesus took hold of Peter completely, his life, his death. Just as on another occasion he had promised to make of him the unshakable Rock of the Church (Mt 16:18-19), he consecrates him today as the Shepherd of the Great Flock. After having invested him with perpetuity, he confers upon him universality. The distinction between lambs and sheep does not seem to single out particularly in the flock of the Christ the faithful and the hierarchy, but simply the totality of the little and the great. The perpetual solidity of the Rock had been linked to firmness of faith, to understanding of the revelation of the mysteries. The universality of the Shepherd is bound to the high quality of love, to the profound reality of adhesion to the very Person of Jesus. But it is quite evident that all of these things should not be separated: in the thought of Jesus, in his plan according to which they are to be realized, they are interdependent.

It is equally evident that such prerogatives and such investitures, if they are indeed of the order of him who gives them, are beyond the measure of the man who receives them. To be the Rock on which will be built the duration of the Church, to be the Shepherd in whose hands is the entire Flock, so extensive as it will become and so numerous as it will be in children and in mothers, is an immense matter. Could Peter, by himself alone, assume such a charge, and attain so great an amplitude? Peter was not immortal; Jesus reminds him of this in an instant. Then, either it must be said that the words of command spoken by Jesus with such solemnity nevertheless did not have very much significance; or it must be admitted that they were of sufficient power to launch, in the religious history of mankind, an enterprise which exceeded the dimensions of one man and of one lifetime, and which presupposed an entire series of men, a succession and transmission of powers, an entire spiritual dynasty.

And, nonetheless, the institution was not founded in the

abstract; everything reposes at first on the person of Peter. It is this small-scale fisherman, intelligent, ardent, religious, receptive, met by Jesus three years earlier at the sea of Tiberias and today rediscovered by him at the same spot, who becomes in effect, as he had promised him, the great fisher of men and shepherd of souls, the first in command after the Christ and the chief of the dynasty. The latter will never be anything but the succession of Peter. When they supervise as good Shepherds the whole Sheepfold of the Christ, when they govern the entire Fishery under the humble sign of the Fisherman, the successors of Peter will do no more than conform with their origin and return to their sources. They will give proof at one and the same time of the greatness and of the humility which are the true marks of all authentic nobility and particularly the marks of theirs. They will be the heirs of Peter. And Peter is the heir of Jesus Christ.

The person of Simon Peter is of such marked importance in this affair that forthwith there is traced the curve of his individual destiny. Through the way in which the Lord speaks to his friend, we grasp that the latter is in between two stages of life: You are no longer young, Jesus tells him, you no longer possess all the vigor of your youth; but neither are you an old man, and I tell you now that after a career that still has a good deal of time to run, you will know in your old age a harsh captivity which will be completely the contrary of the liberty of your youth and will end with a violent death, "you will be borne where you would not go."

The contrast is between the young man who gallantly ties his sash about his waist to freely travel the paths of life, and the fine old man who is brutally bound to be led to death, or rather to be carried thereto, as the text says. If Peter died by crucifixion, the prediction assumes a tragic sense. When John wrote, he knew how his great friend had died; he halfway intimates this, but without extending himself about it any more than he has done for the death of his divine Master. Yet we sense the dawn of an admiration for the glorious martyrdom of Peter, although this is but a parenthetical insertion in the account.

Jesus joined gesture to word: "Follow me," he said to Peter. This was not the first time that Jesus had invited his friends to follow him (Jn 12:26). Peter himself was too ardent a follower not to respond to the appeal (Jn 13:37). If Jesus summoned, he went. And, in fact, there came about then a veritable scene, of a symbolical value whose beauty cannot be sufficiently remarked. The Lord made the gesture of leading his disciple away. The others see the two of them go off to some distance in the morning light; a singular feeling composed of reserve and of respect restrained all of them. Those who were there were sufficiently sensitive to grasp the grandeur of the scene: The Christ drawing Peter away into the mystery! They were equally instructed enough in the divine Power to comprehend that something totally supernatural could be about to happen. Was not the Lord going to take Peter from them? Being able to stand still no longer, John detached himself from the group in order to follow the two who so mysteriously went away.

If he repeats at this moment his most significant titles, this is not merely in order to designate himself a last time at the end of his gospel (although it seems that it may have been somewhat for this motive), but it is also in order to justify his boldness on the occasion and to explain it to the reader. I did not lack the daring, he would appear to say, to want to thus involve myself in the intimacy of the Lord with Peter. Indeed, this had happened to me at other times, especially at the Lord's Supper when from the excellent position I had between Jesus and Peter I posed to Jesus on the part of Peter the sorrowful question which haunted us. John insinuates in this way, with moving lack of sophistication, that he was intimately united to both of them.

The reaction of Peter is also admirable. Going aside with the Lord and seeing John come after them, Peter asks what the future of his young friend will be. Jesus responds by an enigmatic remark, which must have been whetted by a smile and hurled as a gentle mark of defiance. Him? If I will that he not finish with living!

This was the prediction of an extremely long lifetime. Repeated among the disciples, taken literally, such a declaration could receive, to the extent that it was realized, as time went on, a perilous interpretation: John desired to ward this off. Having become quite old, in point of fact the only survivor of the College of the Twelve, known and respected as such in the Churches, he might have passed for being immortal. Besides, he could have been regarded by many as a living annunciation of the approach of the Parousia: in certain milieux, some spirits were terribly vibrant in this expectation. The longevity of John could contribute to leading them astray and to arousing them, bound as it was in the very expression of the Lord to the idea of the Great Return. Finally, once committed to this way, some Christians might award John a superstitious cult; this last error would have been in the eyes of the apostle worse than the others.

John was absolutely desirous that there be no mistake about this point. This is why he gives more precision to the statement that was made, with the result that, when he died, no one was in danger of thinking it false and of being tempted to cut it out of the gospel. John respects the enigma, because it was from the Lord; but he refutes the legend according to which he, the beloved disciple, was not to die, or would survive until the Parousia. The Lord would come, certainly; but it was not the disciple's place to say when.

This account, which is so singularly beautiful, is the last page of the last gospel. With the supreme ease of a very real being who moves about in our sphere and yet has already transcended it, Jesus demonstrates to those who are his that he is himself and that he is indeed Living. This was the third time that he did "this" for them, John observes with admiration in the middle of the account (Jn 21:14); but this time is unprecedented, with mingled condescension and grandeur. Jesus is like a father or mother, who once more finds his orphaned children and forgives them for having so little understood him and for having so thoroughly forsaken him. He is also the leader who reassembles his men on the very spot where he had recruited them, the companion who comes to rejoin his comrades along the path of their work, the most choice of friends, the beloved master, who re-establishes friendship in gentleness and reciprocity.

At the side of Jesus in the luminous lightness of this dawn, Peter stands as a figure of greatness. The gospel of John concludes with a catch of fish by Simon Peter, as that of the synoptics had begun (Mk 1:16-20; Mt 4:18-22; Lk 5:1-11). Only, the circumstances demanding it, John goes far beyond his predecessors: he puts about the forehead of Peter a ray of the glory of Jesus himself. Peter takes on the appearance of the great Fisher of men, the Shepherd of the whole Flock which rallies to the crook of Jesus Christ.

The admirable vision at the end has no end: it closes not with a sudden disappearance but with the limitless perspective in which we see the Lord drawing away into the distance, leading with him Peter and even John to the boundaries of this world and of another, on the banks of time, to the shores of eternity. The evangelist has the gift of introducing us to the most profound of thoughts, without his narration's ceasing to remain simple, familiar, cordial. This gift to the disciple whom Jesus loved, this gift which was so special, was it not that of Jesus himself?

John Testifies to the Facts

The disciples of John, marveling at this inimitable style, must have been enraptured to receive such accounts from the lips of the aged apostle who had been the close friend of Jesus and of Peter. They rejoiced at being able to put them into writing under his dictation. At certain more pathetic or more luminous moments, they bear witness to the authenticity of the testimony; they had the guilelessness to add on their own: "His testimony is truthful," as they wrote when John made known the blow of the lance to the Heart of Jesus (Jn 19:35). They repeat here the same expression, following the final account, as if to place the last period to the entire gospel.

"It was indeed this disciple who bore witness to these things and who has written them, and we know that his testimony is truthful. There were, furthermore, still many other things which Jesus did; they were such that, if they were written one by one, I do not know if the world itself could contain the books that would have to be written" (Jn 21:24-25).

The disciples of John express themselves with greater emphasis than he himself would have done. Perhaps they wished to proclaim through their closing hyperbole not so much the quantity of the things accomplished by Jesus as the divine quality of the works of the Christ. In this case, they are pointing out to the reader that the deeds and the gestures of the Lord were connected to a transcendent order and beyond any proportion with this world. Such a reflection on their part is then something most profound and quite exact: a homage to the grandeur of the Word Incarnate, a homage affixed to the end of John's gospel by faithful disciples as their own epilogue. Hence, in order that there would not be two epilogues following one upon another, it was necessary to remove to a somewhat earlier stage, while at the same time placing it at the least feasible distance, the one which the author had already composed. It is possibly for this reason that this first epilogue, that of John himself, is now placed after the account which comes just before the final one, there where we have studied it (Jn 20:30-31).

CHAPTER 7

THE MISSION OF THE CHURCH

The Mission of the Church According to Matthew

John informs us of the extraordinary conditions on which Jesus manifested himself to Peter and to several of the principal disciples at the sea of Tiberias. To all appearances, this was the beginning of the manifestations in Galilee. Peter was the first alerted, and was fully confirmed in his functions. It was he who received the instructions and transmitted the orders of the Lord. It was he who convoked the other disciples, his brothers of the College, of the Twelve, those who formed a part of the zealous group of the seventy-two, and, in a general manner, all those who could be counted among the faithful.

Paul tells us that the Lord showed himself one day to more than five hundred of the brethren at one time (1 Cor 15:6). Such a gathering could not have been the effect of chance; it had to be occasioned by a convocation. On the other hand, it is conceivable that it could have taken place without hindrance in the Galilean countryside: it was in Galilee that Jesus had the greatest number of disciples and that he had preached the most openly the Reign of God. It was, therefore, there that he could bring together the greatest number of persons, in order to speak to them again of this Reign and to show it to them already marvelously realized in his own Resurrection.

So extensive and so important a demonstration affirmed by Paul and attested by the primitive catechesis, is omitted by the evangelists: this is the proof that they were a long ways from having told everything. Moreover, it is possible that this apparition of such great proportions coincides with that which is recounted by Matthew at the very end of his gospel. He also terminates his gospel in grandeur and in beauty; he loves these great tableaux. He says explicitly that the apparition took place at the mountain which Jesus had designated to them (Mt 28:16).

He mentions, it is true, only the Twelve, because his closing design would have it thus; but nothing precludes many of the disciples having come to join them. Peter along with his colleagues must have assembled the entire people of the new Church. These good people deserved to have the joy of seeing the Lord once more; their love for him would thereby be increased, their faith would be definitively determined. It is also possible that the apparition to the Eleven may have been different from the apparition to the five hundred, since Jesus showed through numerous proofs that he was alive and appeared to them throughout forty days (Ac 1:3).

Matthew has simplified a great deal the entire gospel of the Resurrection. From the moment that he wrote what the enemies of Jesus did immediately after they had heard the report of the guards (Mt 28:11-15), he hastened to write what the friends did after they received the message of the women (Mt 28:16-20). They went at once into Galilee where Jesus had had them informed that he would precede them; this chain of events is logical. The evangelist is not ignorant of the manifestations in Jerusalem: he alludes to the doubts of which at first they were the object (Mt 28:17); but it seemed to him, at the close of his gospel, that the apparition on the mount of Galilee would fittingly bring the work to an end. The mountain, a very specific site, could well have been one of those high places where Jesus had assembled and spoken to his people, the mount of the Beatitudes for example. The Eleven receive their worldwide mission at the very places where they had been called and ordained (Mk 3:13-16 and parallels). Here is the final text of Matthew:

As for the eleven disciples, they betook themselves to Galilee, to the mountain which Jesus had designated to them. From the moment they saw him, they fell prostrate, those who still had doubted. And Jesus drew near to them and spoke to them in these terms: "To me has been given all power in heaven and on earth.

Go, then, instruct all of the nations,
Baptize them in the Name of the Father and of the Son and of the Holy Spirit,
Teach them to keep all that I have prescribed for you.

And behold that I, I am with you, all days, even until the consummation of the world" (Mt 28:16-20).

No reader can be insensible to the grandeur of this scene. Its features are all the more impressive in that they are sober and reduced to the essential. At the mountain to which he had told his own to go, the Lord punctually appeared at the rendezvous: exactness is the courtesy of kings, his was this royal gesture. Matthew does not give the least detail; but the canvas which he sketches allows only majesty to be seen. There is no longer anything of the charming circumstances of the encounter at the edge of the sea; the apparition at the mountain is of a style completely different from that of the apparition at the sea.

It seems that the onlookers saw the Lord coming from afar, from some point of heaven or earth, in symbolical proportion to the Power of which he will speak to them. He comes to them magnificently in an immense gesture of possession and of friendship. No one hesitates this time about his identity. From the moment that they see him and even before he has reached them, the Eleven make before him the profound religious prostration which one makes before God; all imitate them. Imagine the beauty of the sight, if there were there more than five hundred, bowed even to the earth, at the approach of their Lord. Those who at first had doubted the most, the text seems to say, were the most prostrate. The most fervent doubtlessly repeated in loud and

warm voices the words of adoration: My Lord and my God!
And Matthew intimates that the Lord was obliged to lean over
them, to mingle with them in order to lift up all of them from
their prostration and to address to them what he had to declare.

We must gather in the words which Matthew has connected
to this majestic apparition. The greatness of the words is propor-
tioned to the splendor of the apparition. Moreover, each time
that Jesus made himself seen he had something to say; there
were no mute apparitions: this is a trait underlined by all of the
evangelists. The words which Jesus uttered were so perfectly his
that they served to identify him. As previously, he treats of the
establishment of the Reign of God, he speaks of it much more
plainly, like someone who after having come forth from God
has hereafter set out to go back to God (Jn 16:29-30). He affirms
things with a thoroughly simple authority, in a truth that is no
longer of this world: these are not merely words from beyond
the grave, they are words of eternity. In listening to Jesus speak,
as well as in experiencing how he exists, the disciples "see the
Reign of God coming in power" (Mk 9:1), "they have before them
the Son of Man coming into his own Kingdom" (Mt 16:28).

The evangelists have no more reported all of the words
than they have recounted all of the apparitions. But all have been
careful to join some of them to the apparitions which they have
retained. Each has followed the inspiration by which he was
guided. Why these words rather than others? In comparing them
to one another, we perhaps discern better the nature of the in-
tentions which dictated the choice of them and the great meaning possessed by all of them.

Those which we have just read in the narrative of Matthew
can be summed up as three declarations which are, in effect, of
absolutely capital importance and concerning which it was imperative that the disciples have a clear comprehension.

By the first, Jesus affirmed that an "Omnipotence" was
given him in heaven and on earth. We have already heard from
him declarations of this type, particularly in the prayer for Unity
(Jn 17:25). This omnipotence was not new in him, but his Risen

state permitted him to deploy it in its full dimensions and to exercise it in its full strength. It was "given" to him by the Father of whom he was the Envoy, by the God whose man he was. It was given to him "in heaven and on earth": heaven, everything that touches upon God; earth, everything that touches upon man. Jesus was at home in the two domains, because he held within his Person the destiny of man and the grandeur of God. He thus affirmed the sovereign Might of the Man-God. From this Power derived the great mission given by him to his disciples, principally and in the most determined fashion to the Eleven, and the great Presence which he commits himself to grant them in reason of and in proportion to the mandate which he has entrusted to them. All of these words are of the highest import.

The mission is given under the form, which is altogether imperative and operative, of a command to be executed, of a grace which will aid in its execution. This grace will bear the disciples away to the conquest of the world; it will impel them to the spiritual penetration of every nation. The mission is given this time to meet the measure of the Man-God. It is as if Jesus said: Go, go forth from Israel, your first missions were but trials (Mt 10:5-6); take henceforth the path of the Nations, there is not a one which is not to become the field of your sowing and of your harvests (Mt 9:37-38), not a one which cannot furnish sheep for the sheepfold (Mt 9:36; Jn 10:16). Jesus enlarges the horizon of the disciples to the dimensions of mankind. You will do works which will be even greater than those I have done, he had said to them; you will do greater works because you will do them in my total grandeur, that which I have because I go my way to be with my Father (Jn 14:12).

The great works of the mission, Jesus here reduces to three principal tasks. All three have as their aim the elevating of the human race to the level of God. Not just to a vague notion of God, but to a veritable communion with the God who has revealed Himself in such a personal manner in Jesus.

The first work is the task of doctrinal teaching. First of all the Nations must be instructed, the revelations must be made known to them, the mysteries must be preached to them, and, the primary mystery, that of the Name in which they are to be baptized. Spirits must be opened to the light of the Gospel and their faith must be furnished with its true objects, those which Jesus had presented.

The second work ordained by Jesus was a task of sacred impregnation. The human race is not composed of pure spirits; it must have, besides its intellectual initiation, certain sacramental initiations in which the sensible would be the sign and the vehicle of the spiritual; all the nations had looked for the sacred in their rites. Plunge them into water, Jesus solemnly says, baptize them in the Name of the God which you will teach them; thus bring about their rebirth through water and through the Spirit: this will be their fashion of entering into the Kingdom of Heaven (Jn 3:5). This first bath will purify them spiritually, will cleanse them from sin; this first sacrament will lead them to the others.

The third work incorporated into the order of the mission is again one of teaching, but more oriented toward the practical: Teach them to keep all that I have commanded you. The commandments of Jesus, as everyone ought to know by the end of the Gospel, are not merely directed to a moral life, clean and proper in every way; they are also directed to a profound theological life, in which man is called upon to go back into his heart and there commune with God.

Jesus could have added several words of explanation or of application to these noble imperatives in which are briefly inscribed his dearest institutions and his most profound thoughts. In any event, he projected sufficient light into their minds that the disciples were able to understand clearly what he wanted: "The hour is coming," he had said to them, "when I shall converse with you in plain terms" (Jn 16:25). It had come: He proclaimed his word, and the Church finds here unto perpetuity the charter of its mission.

On the interior of the great mission, the great presence. The two are of the same order and possess the same dimension. Like the mission, the presence is in proportion to the power of the risen Jesus. It is not easy to define in clear concepts this presence of the Christ in his Church and in his faithful; but it is promulgated and promised in the most formal of terms, terms which are most expressive and most extensive.

Jesus says: "I am with you, all the days that God will make, even to the consummation of the world," even to that day when time will run out. "You," these are all the disciples, not only the leaders, but also the small, the lesser people of the Christ. "I am": there is here first of all the great affirmation of existence heard several times on the lips of Jesus. "With you," he says: not only when you are together, in a collectivity, in a society, or when you are several united in my Name (Mt 18:20); but also when it is the pleasure of any one of you to retire into the secrecy of your heart (Mt 6:4, 6, 18).

Jesus attributes equal omnipresence to his omnipotence. Beneath this "I" which is so affirmative, "I, with you," whom does he designate? Evidently his Person. But such as it is in God, or such as it is in the Man-God? If it is as God that Jesus promises to be present, there is no difficulty and no novelty in what he says. God is everywhere, nothing escapes his power, nor the sight of his spirit, nor the empire of all that he is; such ubiquity is proper to him, undeniably, inalienably, incommunicably.

But it is not only thus, it is through his faculties as Man that Jesus renders himself present. He speaks here as the Head and yet as a friend, he remains a brother among brothers. In reintegrating the glory which was his before the world was, he does not abdicate his human nature; he carries it, on the contrary, to the highest degree of power and of presence. It is to this sacred Humanity, assumed by him and now glorified in him, that he awards the prerogative of universal and perpetual presence.

This presence, as associated as it is to that of God, still will not equal it. The substance of the Man-God is not endowed with ubiquity: being body and soul, it is quite necessary that it be somewhere, it cannot be everywhere. It is in itself a great deal, we might say in passing, that he extends a real presence to every point at which he makes his Body and his Blood exist. And the omnipresence which his human substance cannot have, to an immense extent he attains and compensates for by his great knowledge and power as a man. Neither are this knowledge and this power equal to those of God: no created spirit can equal the divine Spirit; but human intelligence possesses in Jesus a singular grandeur and it is thereby that he is so present.

This presence of the Christ in the society of the Church and even in the intimate depths of the soul became immediately for Christians a truth of the first order, one by which they were intensely penetrated. Everything recounted in the book of the Acts breathes of this presence. The New Testament is filled by it: as much as the presence of Yahveh dominates the whole of the Old, just so much that of Jesus dominates the whole of the New.

In the letters to the seven Churches at the debut of the Apocalypse, the Son of Man, become the glorious Christ, is invested with the most extraordinary prerogatives of presence and of power. He holds the seven Churches in his hands; he can at his pleasure extinguish, intensify or rekindle the flame in them; he is the Alpha and the Omega of all; he drives in the two-edged sword; he sounds the mind and the heart; he gives to eat of the fruit of the tree of life; he distributes the Spirit of God; he writes the names in the Book of Life; he is the faithful and truthful witness; he stands at the door (that is, at the door of the soul) and he knocks; if anyone hears his voice and opens the door, the Christ enters into his home, dines with him, becomes his most intimate guest and, in the end, has this disciple who has conquered sit upon the throne where he himself is seated with the Father (Rv 2-3).

In the thought of the writer, all of these metaphors signify realities: John writes all this in an effort to present a vivid image of that presence with which the entire Church is impregnated. These and all the other extremely varied expressions of which the New Testament makes use say nothing more than what has been affirmed by Jesus himself and demonstrated by him in the experiences of his admirable Ascension.

Let us put ourselves in the place of the disciples and feel the tremendous faith being born in them. Their Lord is no longer in any particular place, and yet he is everywhere; they do not know where to situate him; he might spring up at any spot in the fields, at the corner of any street, in any room of any house; he might direct his speech to any purpose. Each of them says to himself: I indeed know that he sees me, I keenly sense that he helps me, I can have no secret from him, he is in me more myself than am I.

Of this presence, no one can say where it begins or where it ends; it cannot be bound by the limits of time or of space; it has the gift of passing through everything, bodies cannot oppose to it their impenetrability, nor spirits their innermost realm; and, although remaining a human presence, it appears to be invested with a divine power. The disciples had experienced these marvelous gifts. The Lord had presented himself without anything having been able to stand in his way. He knew the condition of each soul. Thomas did not have to reveal to him the exigencies of his critical thought; nor Peter, the tenderness of his love for him.

When they reflected upon this strange penetration of the Christ among his own, it appeared to them to be modeled upon the divine presence and seemed to them to be the instrument of this very presence. Jesus had put them on the track toward this comparison when he had pronounced words like these: "O Father, that they may be in me and that I may be in them, as you yourself are in me and I in you" (Jn 15:10, 17:10, 21).

Assuredly, it is God who gives to his Christ the means to be thus extended, in his Church, to everything and to everyone. But for his part, the Christ furnishes God with the incomparable means of touching mankind and of there transforming the divine presence of immensity into a presence of intimacy, the presence of creation into a presence of indwelling: "If anyone loves me," Jesus had said, "we shall come to him and we shall make our abode with him" (Jn 14:23). The presence of the Christ renders God nearer, better known and better loved. When Jesus promises to maintain it throughout all time in his Church, when he gives to his faithful, as he does here, the assurance and the pledge of it, he engages himself toward them in a commitment of which they will always have the right to remind him.

He equally formulates a prophecy which will forever be capable of verification. The world itself and those who, like it, see things from the exterior, can observe that throughout all the vicissitudes of its history, even and above all at the most troubled hours, the Church has found its consistency and placed its reliances upon the Christ: the perennial character of the institution is a good indication of the solidness of its foundation, and also of the realness of the presence of guardianship promised and accorded.

For those who see things and appreciate them from within, the observation is still more impressive: the deepest life of the soul in the Christian Church can only be explained through the permanent action of Jesus. The holy assembly of souls, their society in faith, hope and charity, is totally steeped in the presence of the Christ; at the same time, the Church is the conservator and the shelter of the revelation of God such as it has been effected in the Christ. Always the understanding of the believers has perceived therein the divine Persons as Jesus had made them known. Always in the Church the Christian heart has loved God as Jesus taught it to love him: it loves God tenderly, as a Father; the beloved Son alone can make him thus loved; if he does this, it is because he is there.

The Mission of the Church, According to Mark

The words related in Matthew depict things with a great deal of majesty and with a keen accent of personalness. We have in the conclusion of Mark another version of similar words. This termination, written by the pen of an inspired apostle or disciple of the Lord, has been added to the unfinished gospel of Mark without anyone's even having been preoccupied with smooth-

ing over the joint. This kind of way of doing things is quite un-
affected and merits confidence; it denotes respect for the unfinished text and for the added text.

The latter has nothing of the quaintness of Mark; it does
not give a precise and detailed view of things, but an abridgement without nuances of time or of place, a schematic summary
of the events in which abstraction is made from the circumstances
surrounding them. From the apparition to Magdalene, we are
taken in a single stroke and as if by flight, straight to the Ascension; we see in a single tableau what the Lord did among his
own, with the women, with those who were simply disciples,
with the Eleven, in this Ascension. There is no preciseness, except for the words reported (Mk 16:15-18); it is this which points
to a foreign hand, for customarily in Mark the events occupy
more place than do the words. We regard, then, those which
have been consigned in the conclusion added to Mark's gospel.

> And he said to them: "Go into the whole world to preach
> the gospel to every creature. He who believes and receives
> baptism will be saved; but he who will not believe will be
> condemned. Furthermore, certain signs will accompany
> those who believe; behold them: In my Name, they will
> expel demons, they will speak new tongues; they will even
> take serpents in their hands and any deadly poison they
> might drink will do them no harm; they will lay their hands
> on the sick, and the latter will find themselves well."
> He, the Lord Jesus, after he had said this to them, was
> taken up to heaven and went to take his seat at the right
> hand of God.
> As for them, they went to preach everywhere, the Lord
> however being at work with them, and giving his support
> to the Word through the miracles which accompanied it
> (Mk 16:15-20).

This command to the mission and the tableau connected to
it have a more abstract twist and are less personal than in Matthew, but they remain quite beautiful all the same, and are of
equal greatness. In relation to Mark himself, this tableau which

was a later addition ought not to be judged as if it were from the same stream as that which preceded it. There is a certain incoherence in the fact that Mark acknowledges the rendezvous in Galilee (Mk 16:7), while the author of the conclusion does not situate the command to the mission in Galilee at all. As this writer relates neither date nor place, nothing precludes that the words conserved by him, might be brought together with those which have been reported by Matthew as having been said on the mount of Galilee.

The mission is presented with just as much extension and still more domain than in Matthew. It is offered to the entire world: it is addressed to the whole human race, but through it it reaches all creation. Jesus does not tell how all creation can be touched, indeed transformed, by the establishment of the new Reign. However, there is here an affirmation whose point we must not blunt, and whose mystery we can only respect; the Church and the Gospel which it is to propagate throughout the world have the efficacy of the Man-God. Nor does Jesus say what the duration of the era of propagation will be or what will be its success. The declaration which follows allows it to be understood that this success will not be complete: the Man-God is not more mighty than God, he is only his incomparable Instrument.

By this title he is without equal: there is no mediator above him, no salvation outside of him; he cannot be surpassed or even equalled in his Task or in his Person. The works of the Christ, as Jesus so often repeated, are the very achievement of God, a kind of divinization of creatures added precisely to their creation. But, at the very heart of this task to which the Word Incarnate is vowed, there is a mystery which Jesus has not lifted and which abides, as he has said, as the secret of the Father (Mk 13:32; Mt 24:36).

We find once again, in the text adjoined to Mark, Faith and Baptism: spiritual initiation is accompanied by sacramental initiation, the latter being the sign and the instrument of the former. Both are proposed as the primordial element of the Christian institution, and the initial object of the mission in the world. This conclusion agrees with that of Matthew. It recalls, besides, the supreme alternative preached by Jesus, salvation or damnation, as a capital consequence of the Christian message, deriving from the sovereign importance of this message: the men who reject the Christ reject God.

Paul draws from this several urgent considerations concerning the necessity of the Christian apostolate. Faith, he says, is born of preaching, of the command given by the Christ (Rm 10:12-17). One single excuse is possible: either I have not been told, or I have not truly grasped what I have been told; but the apostle Paul esteems that this excuse is not valid for everyone (Rm 10:18-21).

To the command to the mission is annexed the promise of signs which will accompany its execution. It is the gift of miracles which is thus promised, not to such or such a disciple in particular, nor even to such and such a category, but to the collectivity, and more specially to those of the faithful who will be employed in the mission. It is promised in view of this mission, in order to single it out to the world, in order to give it prestige and authority. Jesus means to say that this gift of miracles will never be totally missing from his Church. He obtains and offers it as one of the signs of his presence, not the only one, nor the most important nor the most intimate, but, when need arises, the most sensational.

The different miracles are classified according to a canvas of expediency, which must be interpreted rather broadly and perhaps also in a spiritual sense, indeed even a symbolical sense. The first signs are precisely those which touch closest upon the things of the spirit; the last, those concerned with the protecting of life and the care of the body itself. Take for example the gift of expelling demons: it is probable that it comprises not only the faculty of exorcising the possessed but also the privilege of mastering the diabolical Powers and of influencing spirits, in freeing them, in enlightening them. In the miracle of new tongues, it is permissible to see the gift of elucidating the sacred mysteries and of harmoniously exposing the major objects of faith, or again the gift of reading souls or of penetrating the future. The gift of giving health to the body will sometimes go as far as bringing it back to life. These miraculous powers, if over-abundantly exercised, would deflect the work of the Christ from its true path; but, well placed, providentially handled, they contribute to singling it out.

The tableau which comes after the word of Jesus and which closes the gospel establishes a contrast between the Ascension of the Lord to heaven and the dispersion of the disciples over the earth. He ascends to take his seat at the right hand of God. They depart in all directions to fulfill the task of preaching. The first proposition is a homage to the Christ; the author seems to say: This unique repose at the right of God, Jesus indeed merited! This, furthermore, is not the expression of an historian, but of a theologian, a dogmatic formula stating a thought of faith in metaphorical terms of which Jesus himself must have made use (Mk 14:62). The metaphor is simple, everyone can hear it. He who sits at the right hand of the Great King is the man who comes the first after him: confidences are entrusted to him, his are the secrets of the Reign; he shares in the honors; he partakes of the glory of the Prince himself, is associated to all of the enterprises of the Kingdom, is the prime minister and the right hand of the King. This was a manner of expressing the excellence and the grandeur of the Man-God and his state of glory in the nearness of God. It was adopted in the symbols of faith. It has its place in the Gospel.

This matter of sitting at the right of God, far from constituting an obstacle to presence in the Church, a presence so solemnly promised according to Matthew, is the pledge and guarantee of it. It is because the Lord Jesus is so thoroughly established in the Godhead, that he is able to be at work with the disciples wherever they are and able to give support to all that they do, principally to their more spiritual activity, the diffusion of the Truth by means of the Word. The sign of this support of the Christ here is that of the accompanying miracles: this final notation is in harmony with what was said in the command to the mission, but it does not pretend to be exclusive; there are a good many other signs of the presence of the Christ in his Church. Without harmonizing completely, the first two gospels join one another apropos to this presence: one recalls the promise of it (Mt 28:20); the other evokes its realization (Mk 16:20).

The Mission of the Church According to Luke

Neither has Luke, for his part, failed to add to the account of the apparitions a compendium of teachings. Those which he reports are also of prime importance. Yet, for one thing, they are different from those which the preceding evangelists have related. In Luke, after Jesus has plainly shown to the disciples that he has risen, he speaks to them; he desires that they also recognize him through his words.

> Now, he said to them, "These, then, are my teachings, those which I formulated in addressing you while I was still with you. I said to you: There must be accomplished everything which has been written with regard to me, in the Law of Moses and in the Prophets and in the Psalms." It was then that he opened their understanding so that they might be able to grasp these Scriptures. "Ah yes," he said to them, "behold indeed what is written: the Christ must suffer, then rise from among the dead the third day, then, there must be preached in his Name repentance in view of the remission of sins, it must be preached to all nations, beginning however with Jerusalem... You are the witnesses of this... And behold, I send forth upon you the promise of my Father; but keep your place in this City until you are clothed with the Strength from on High" (Lk 24:44-49).

This fragment is of considerable import: Jesus himself gives to his disciples a more profound understanding of the Scriptures. Luke, however, has not been the evangelist who has shown himself the most concerned about supporting the events which he records by the prophecies which had announced them; Matthew preoccupied himself with this much more: the present passage would be most comprehensible in his text. Nevertheless, Luke was not ignorant of the Scriptures, he had a great love for his Greek Bible; perhaps even, in writing, he felt himself inclined to imitate it. Moreover, he was aware of the importance assumed in Christian preaching by the interpretation of Scripture; he admired the authority which had been acquired in this matter by the masters of interpretation: Peter, Paul and the others; and this was why he saw fit to recall at the end of his gospel how the divine Master in person had put the disciples on this track. This feature already noted in the conversation with the two from Emmaus (Lk 24:26-27) is here pointed out more explicitly, and presented among the last teachings of Jesus.

According to Luke, it was from Sion that the new Law should come forth, in Jerusalem that the first preaching should take place; yet, the latter was entrusted to young Galileans who were certainly not masters in Israel. How could they, from the debut of their apostolate, in the city of the great schools and face to face with the great doctors, make use of the Scriptures with more authority than the latter and with so much lucidity, so much penetration, if Jesus had not given them the Spirit to do so and shown them the way? The fragment reproduced by Luke is quite in line with the needs of the situation.

Jesus spoke to his disciples, as if it was a question of an encounter with them henceforth growing late: "When I was with you," he said to them. Did this mean that the days of the manifestation had about run out? Or, did this remark indicate change of state more than duration of time? For, from the first moments of his Resurrection, Jesus could already say in all truth: The time when I was with you! Such is probably the nuance.

The grandeur of the entire passage comes from the fact that it unites in a single view the consideration of the past and that of the future. All of the past is to be reviewed, Jesus said to his disciples; you must study all of your Bible anew. He obligingly enumerates its three divisions, the principal scrolls: the Law, the

Prophets, the Psalms. He makes it understood that these Scriptures are the expression of a divine plan. They concern the person of the Messiah and the whole of the propaganda which ought to be borne to the nations by the true Messianism, that which obtains the real goods of the soul, those goods which come from God and which lead back to God, sins pardoned, grace bestowed. Jesus had to teach his disciples to rethink the Scriptures in function of him and of his Task; the principal articles of the new faith, which will become the object of the initial catechesis and constitute the Creed of the Apostles, are thus connected to the Scripture of old.

Paul repeats, as a lesson learned, formulae of this type (1 Cor 15:34). If they imposed themselves so quickly and so deeply on the thought of the first Christians, was this not because they were in reference precisely to the very teachings of Jesus? He had opened their understanding, as the text says, and poured a great deal of light into their spirit. The great things to come, the perspective of which he sketches, he invites them to see in the context of that entire past of prefigurations and of prophecies, which was their own, that of their fathers, the religious history of their nation. You are the witnesses of all this, he concludes munificently. That is, of the prefiguration which took place in the past, of the realization which has come about in the present, and of the continuation which it will have in the future. The disciples are in an incomparable position, at the crossroads of the two Testaments. They are the representatives of the Old; they have it in their blood. They are the pioneers of the New: Jesus makes this a part of their spirit. And we see them consecrated by the Christ himself as his very special witnesses.

The last two phrases of the teaching consigned in Luke are related to the measures which the Lord in fact must have taken at the termination of his Ascension. The conclusion of Mark also finishes with a tableau of the same sort, in a contrast between Jesus and his own. Only, the situations are reversed: in Mark, Jesus goes to take his place and the disciples are set into motion; in Luke, it is the inverse, Jesus says: If I go away, it is in order to

send to you what my Father has promised; but you, do not make
a move until you are invested with the Strength from on High.
However, the two tableaux fit together very well: the movement
of the Lord Jesus bears him away to an Enthronement which is
to endure for eternity; the repose of the disciples prepares them
for the mission whose prolongation will be that of the world's.

"The City" is Jerusalem. The account of Luke has not departed from it. In point of fact, near the end of the forty days,
Jesus must have brought back from Galilee the caravan of his
principal disciples. For him, the journey did not count: the Man-
God was no longer a traveler on earth. For those who were about
to dedicate themselves to perpetual wandering, this one journey
was nothing. Furthermore, Pentecost was approaching, and after the Pasch this was the feast for which they were most willing
to set everything else aside. "The Promise of the Father," "the
Strength from on High," this was the Holy Spirit, the Paraclete.
The disciples had only to "await him": they would be "clothed"
with him, spiritually armed, equipped, strengthened by him,
after Jesus had left them. The gospel of Luke has not reported
that Jesus had made on the part of the Father the Promise of the
Holy Spirit; this gap is filled in in the gospel of John.

The Mission of the Church According to John

The teachings of Jesus retained by John in the gospel of the
Resurrection are not numerous but are quite memorable, and of
the most noteworthy importance. We remember the words spoken to Peter, to consecrate him the Shepherd of the whole Flock
(Jn 21:15-17), then to announce to him his martyrdom, while
enhancing all this with the "Follow me" in which the Lord makes
the gesture of leading Peter away with him (Jn 21:18-19). We
remember another declaration and another gesture which were
the act of a great rabbi passing on to those who were to continue
him his spirit and his powers. This was a scene of capital impor-

tance. The evangelist has incorporated it into the account of the apparition on the evening of the Pasch, but there is nothing to indicate that in fact it was connected thereto; the conjunction and the adverb at the beginning rather give the impression of a separate scene, which we regard in its curtailed form.

> Therefore another time he said to them: "Peace to you. As the Father has sent me, I also send you." Then, after having said this, breathing upon them, he declared to them: "Accept the Holy Spirit: whose sins you remit, they will be remitted; whose you retain, they will be retained" (Jn 20:21-23).

This appears to be a kind of final act by which the Lord takes possession of those who are his before taking leave of them. The mission is evoked in this text of John's as broadly as it was in Mark or in Matthew. It is compared to that of Jesus. It is no longer measured by its extent, its duration, its effects, as in the other statements, but by its origin, one could almost say: by its divine procession. The mission which the Church receives from the Christ is connected to that which the Son receives from the Father, just as the union of the members of this Church among themselves and with the Christ is bound to that of the Son with the Father and the Three Persons in God.

Faithfully gathered in by John, thoughts of this kind have been inscribed in the discourse after the Supper (Jn 15:10, 15; 17:18, 23); it is not astonishing that there is a reminder of them in the discourse of the Ascension. It is this entire mystery of suffering and of glory, of death and of resurrection, which determines in effect the departure on the mission and constitutes the first news of the new Reign.

The gesture of the Lord is purely symbolical, sacramental in a way, but sovereignly significant. Even in his glorious state, Jesus did not disdain the humble signs of which we stand in need. He breathed upon his disciples, to better open the way for the word which he spoke and also the reality which it bore with it. This breath of Christ was no doubt also the image of the Spirit. Jesus had compared the Spirit to the breath of a great wind (Jn 3:8). On Pentecost, the coming of the Spirit will be singled out by a violent blowing of the wind (Ac 2:2). Here it is more simple, but how much more stirring! It is the breath of the Risen One signifying the communication of the Holy Spirit.

In the conciseness of John's text the gesture of breathing probably is related to what preceded and to what follows; it forms the bond between the high mission which is conferred and the Holy Spirit who is communicated. Does it not suggest another symbolism? The Lord Jesus breathing a new spirit into the humanity which he had come to save, is this not a reminder of the Lord Yahveh breathing the first breath of the spirit into the man formed from the dust of the earth (Gn 2:7)?

The mission cannot be conceived apart from the communication of the Holy Spirit. The gesture makes it understood that this Holy Spirit had already been given. This did not preclude his still being promised, for he was to be given even much more abundantly after Jesus had completely returned to the side of the Father. At the end of Luke's gospel we have found an allusion to this promise and the formal command to wait for it to be fulfilled; in the gospel of John, in the course of the conversations of the Last Supper, it is expressed as many as five times (Jn 14:16, 26, 15:26, 16:7, 13). The Holy Spirit is now invoked not with regard to effusions to come, but for a communication which was very much of the moment; it is not a question here of a promise being recalled, but of a presence being realized. Jesus does not say: You will receive; he says: Receive the Holy Spirit; as if to forcefully signify: Grasp him, I give him to you, I breathe him into you, hold him tightly; his presence is essential to the power which I grant you.

This power, according to Matthew, had already been promised by Jesus, to Peter first of all (Mt 16:19), then to the other disciples (Mt 18:18): it is the power of binding and of releasing in view of Heaven, of opening or of shutting the entrance to the Kingdom, the power of the Keys. John is desirous of making it known that the Lord, before leaving the disciples, granted it to them in fact, through a solemn transmission, in the days of his Ascension. The expression of it is even clearer in the bestowal than in the promise. Jesus had spoken at first in metaphors; the hour had come when he spoke openly (Jn 16:25): When you remit someone's sins, they will be remitted, when you retain them, they will be retained.

We read indeed in Luke that the preaching which is to take place in the name of the Christ to all the nations must be orientated toward the remission of sins (Lk 24:47). John's passage goes much further: it is not only a way of preaching that Jesus entrusts to his disciples, but a jurisdiction which he confers upon them, for the remission of sins. They have more to do than preach repentance; they have to effect it in a certain sense. They are not only charged with an instruction to be addressed to the mind, but with a government over souls, with a power of directing consciences and of setting them aright.

The assignment which some of the ancient prophets in their turn, and John the Baptist still more recently (Lk 3:10-14; Jn 1:23), had carried out zealously and sometimes successfully fulfilled, according to the nature of the inspiration which was given them, we now see Jesus elevating to the rank of a sacred institution and a permanent function. "Just as my Father, for my sake, has placed at my disposal a Kingdom, I, for your sake, place it at your disposal," he said to his friends. "You will eat at my table, you will occupy the thrones and you will judge the twelve tribes of Israel," of the new Israel (Lk 22:29-30). When Jesus spoke of his own Kingdom (Mt 13:41), it was of his Church that he was talking. He makes his declaration: He does that which he had promised. He invests the Great Ones of the Kingdom with a veritable spiritual magistracy. Among other things, and in relation to an important part of their mission, he constitutes them Judges. But, no more than the Kingdom is of this world, is the Judgeship made to pronounce sentence concerning the affairs of this world. It has the meaning and the efficacy of a sacrament: it produces completely spiritual effects and is directed to nothing less than the liberation of souls from sin in administering grace to them.

This sacred tribunal continues the work of the Christ: it looks to the purification of consciences, to their punishment if necessary, but above all to healing them, to contributing to their growth, to reestablishing them in the intimacy of God, to causing them to prosper and fructify therein; the sentences have wherewith to bestow upon souls the life with God. Such a power cannot operate without the Holy Spirit; this is why Jesus said to his own: "Take hold of the Holy Spirit," and breathed him into them. He thus passes on to his Great Ones, beneath the shepherd's crook of Peter, the Keys to the Kingdom. The Gospel, whether that of John or of the others, leaves no doubt about the nature of these Keys and of this Kingdom.

We might be surprised that John does not report any more words than these in his gospel of the Resurrection. It is permissible to surmise that he has inserted several of these noteworthy declarations in the discourse after the Supper. The invitations to the house of the Father (Jn 14:1-11), the revelations concerning the dwelling of the divine Persons in the heart of the disciples (Jn 14:12-26), the profound considerations of the prayer for Unity (Jn 17), these are some of the Words of the Ascension. Everyone can have for himself the experience of rereading them from this perspective.

CHAPTER 8

THE ASCENSION

The Lord Taken Away to Heaven

The four gospels come to an end with the Ascension which itself is dated from the Resurrection. The final words in Matthew make an indirect allusion to it. When Jesus declares to his disciples that he is with them at all times and among all nations until the consummation of the world, we understand that he is no longer of this world and that his assistance comes to us from the side of God (Mt 28:20).

In Mark the closing fragment alludes directly to the Ascension, yet without giving the least detail: "The Lord Jesus having been taken away to Heaven, went to take his seat at the right of God" (Mk 16:19). Heaven here designates the radiation of God among his most choice creatures, in the material universe, and even more so in the spiritual realm, in which takes place the vision of God, communion in his life.

To say that Jesus was taken away to Heaven, was to say that through his body he henceforth occupied in creation a site and a situation worthy of him. Extracted from the conditions of our tiny globe, the glorious body of Jesus was not taken out of the whole of the Cosmos. Without being constrained or measured by this vast habitat, It reigns sovereignly over it, it is the center constituting it, its principle and its measure. It is at the heart of the creations of God, the Alpha and the Omega of the new heaven, since It is the sacred Body of the Word of God, of the Word in whom everything is made, in whom everything holds together. The Ascension of Jesus is an event of cosmic import.

There is more. To say that Jesus was taken away to Heaven, was to say that his great soul had been transported to the womb of God. Doubtlessly, at the summit of its spiritual powers, it had never ceased to see God nor to rejoice in him. But, by its involvement in the midst of us, neither did it fail to take part in our activities, to experience in total sincerity our ways of thinking and of loving, of feeling and of acting. It is the whole of this deployment which knew on this day its supreme flourishing and received its reward. In this participation in the intimate life of the Godhead, the soul of Jesus was elevated to the most eminent degree conceivable; it was this that the disciples meant where they professed that their Lord had gone "to be seated at the right of God."

At the end of the fourth gospel, there is no allusion to the Ascension, unless from the deeply mysterious perspective which terminates the account of the apparition to Peter and to John (Jn 21:20-23). On the other hand, several clear allusions can be read at the conclusion of the talk on the Bread of life (Jn 6:62) and in the discourse and the prayer following the Supper (Jn 14, 17): it is therefrom that the theologian of the Ascension can draw the most helpful elements.

The Account of Luke

Luke ought to be considered as the historian of the Ascension: he is the only one to recount the mystery from the viewpoint wherein it had been perceptible to experience. We have two accounts of the facts, the first in abridged form, at the end of the gospel, the second in more detailed form, at the debut of the book of the Acts.

This is the first:

Afterwards, Jesus led his disciples out to Bethany. Then he raised his hands and blessed them. And this happened: While he was blessing them, he was separated from them; he was taken away to heaven. As for them, after they had prostrated themselves before him, they went back to Jerusalem in great joy; and they were steadfastly in the Temple to bless God (Lk 24:50-53).

In the second account Luke seems to have wished to make up for the briefness of the first by setting the event itself even more within the circumstances which preceded or followed it. He sketches this tableau:

To tell the truth, in the first work which I have composed, O Theophilus, concerning everything that Jesus undertook to do and to teach, I continued the composition up to the day on which, after having given his orders, through the Holy Spirit, to the apostles whom he had chosen, he was taken away. It was also to them that he personally presented himself, after his Passion, giving evidence by many proofs that he was indeed alive: during forty days, he was seen by them, and he spoke of the affairs of the Kingdom of God. Then, after he had so thoroughly united himself to them again [that is: to the extent of sharing their table and of eating with them], he enjoined them not to go far from Jerusalem but to wait there for the fulfillment of the Promise of the Father, "that of which you have heard me speak," he said, "for John himself baptized only in water, but you, you will be baptized in the Holy Spirit, and this is but a few days away."
They therefore, in going out with him [it is implied: to the place to which he was leading them], were asking questions; they demanded [we can surmise: among other things]: "Lord, is it at this time that you are going to restore the Royalty for the sake of Israel?" He retorted in addressing them: "It is not your business to know the times or the moments which the Father has determined by his own authority. On the other hand, at the coming of the Holy Spirit upon you, you will receive strength and you

will thus be my witnesses in Jerusalem first of all, then
throughout Judea, in Samaria itself and even to the ends
of the earth."
When he had said this, he was taken away as they watched;
then, a cloud came to shut him off from their eyes. And, as
they were there holding their gaze fixedly toward the sky
while he was going away, behold, two men in white gar-
ments made themselves present in the midst of them. And
indeed, they said: "Men of Galilee, why do you remain
looking at the sky? This same Jesus who from your midst
has just been taken away to heaven will thus come again,
in the same manner as you have seen at his departure for
heaven."
Then they returned to Jerusalem from the Mount of Olives, which is near Jerusalem, at the distance of a Sabbath's
journey. And, when they had come back, they went up to
the upper room, which was their usual dwelling. There
were Peter and John, and James and Andrew, Philip and
Thomas, Bartholomew and Matthew, James of Alpheus
and Simon the Zealot and Judas of James. All of these per-
severed with one and the same heart in prayer, along with
the women and Mary the mother of Jesus, and also with
the brothers of Jesus (Ac 1:1-14).

This second tableau completes the first. Both of them summarize the situations more than they describe particular incidents. At the beginning of the Acts, Luke corrects what had been
too crowded together at the end of his gospel: the manifestation
of the Lord had lasted forty days, and it had donned many forms.
Jesus had "reunited with his apostles" even to the point of once
more sitting at table with them in order to better mark, numerous times, it would seem, the recovery of life and the resump-
tion of contact.

If the evangelical account presents, as witnesses of the facts,
other disciples along with the Eleven, it nevertheless gives to the
latter a place apart (Lk 24:33). It is not astounding that they are
next mentioned alone with their title of Apostles at the inception
of the book which is consecrated to them (Ac 1:2), although a

little farther on the text explicitly says that the other disciples are not excluded (Ac 1:14).

A difference which is regarded as suspect by the critics is that which the apparition of the angels imprints upon the account. Yet, it cannot be said that the latter is so wondrous, the other aspects are not particularly striking, nor to the honor of the disciples, such as the question they pose. The author has no intention of depicting the event with great splendor; from this respect, the tableau coming from his brush in the Gospel is already of unequaled majesty; in the Acts he simply records the facts with more detail, as he had been told that they happened.

The Ascension had only been perceptible in its point of departure, its point of arrival was in another world. Luke does not endeavor to describe the mystery. He makes use of three verbs in order to designate it, as if he hesitated as to which was the best, but all three are quite simple: he says that Jesus was "taken away" from them (Ac 1:2, 11), that he was "lifted up" in their sight as in a solemn flight (Ac 1 :9), that he was "borne" on high (Lk 24:51). Luke has left the three verbs in the passive doubtlessly to better emphasize that the cause of this Ascension was in the divine strength by which the sacred Humanity of Jesus was filled.

According to the second account of Luke, in his various manifestations to the disciples the Lord "reunited himself with them" as if he had again lived among them. John furnishes an example of this in the apparition to several of them at the sea of Tiberias (Jn 21:1-14). Peter alludes to such intimacies when he declares emotionally: "We ate and drank with him after his Resurrection from among the dead" (Ac 10:41). And it is in calling to mind in a view of the whole the experiences of this kind that the account of Luke moves along towards the very last experiences. What the Lord had repeated throughout forty days, one day he repeats for the last time.

Only at the end is there any indication of the places which formed the theater and the persons who were the witnesses of these final revelations. We learn that everything happened in the Holy City and its nearest suburb, no farther down the road than a person had the right to journey on a Sabbath's day, scarcely a mile. The departure of Jesus took place at the Mount of Olives (Ac 1:12); at the end of the gospel it is simply written that Jesus led his disciples out towards Bethany (Lk 24:50).

The Upper Room

The text of the Acts also informs us that upon returning to the town, the witnesses of the Ascension mounted to the upper room where they were accustomed to meet together. It was, then, there that the Lord had reassembled them after having brought them back from Galilee. It was there that he came to spend precious moments with them. It is not certain nor even probable that this upper chamber was that of the Lord's Supper. The Cenacle was a beautiful room upstairs in a wealthy home. The term of which Luke makes use here is different: it designates a construction on a terrace, generally a vast room, not always very ornate or well enclosed, but quite isolated from the movement of the street and because of this convenient for meetings dedicated to prayer or instruction. Some rabbis would thus hold school on the roofs. It was in a setting such as this that the Lord must have regrouped his own. What would happen at these supreme moments? If Luke takes the trouble of writing about this with some solemnity, this is the proof that he was informed and that he attached importance to this clustering together.

The evangelist once more presents here the list of the apostles. There they are, the entire Eleven, who had remained or again become faithful. The forty days had brought to completion their adhesion to the Person and to the Task of Jesus; he was henceforth their Lord and their God. They appear to be grouped according to their affinities in regard to him: first, the four closest friends, those in whom he principally confided, Peter at the head as always, and John very closely bound to him, then their two brothers; next, inscribed two by two, Philip and Thomas, Bartholomew and Matthew: versed in the ancient teachings, they had not failed to open their understanding to the new doctrine, disputing it temporarily, and ultimately accepting it fully; in last place, the representatives of the family, who had been wise enough to join to kinship according to the flesh kinship according to the spirit.

The gospel of Luke has given certain roles to the women. There were some who were present at the last manifestations of Jesus. No doubt the same ones who had come back from Galilee one more time (Lk 24:10) with the disciples, together with those from Jerusalem and its environs, and the friends from Bethany. They had with them Mary, the mother of Jesus; this presence is the indication of the greatness of the events.

"The brothers of Jesus," that is: relatives other than those who formed a part of the Apostolic College, they also represented the family. Perhaps they were there in a kind of official way, summoned by Jesus himself, as if he desired, in making them witnesses of his Ascension, to attest to the sincerity of his Incarnation and to give this mark of recognition to the entire clan which had been his on this earth. The presence of the brothers of Jesus has in these circumstances a profoundly human character. We can think that these relatives of more or less close kinship had become believers, at least when they had seen Jesus in his Resurrection.

This unusual and, in spite of everything, rather disparate assembly recalls that which has been singled out by John at the beginnings of the public life (Jn 2:12). Thus, the manifestation of Jesus finished as it had begun, before the same witnesses; but a difference exists and it is significant: in the first instance the brothers were named before the disciples, while the last time they are named afterwards. The spiritual bonds have prevailed over the bonds of the flesh; and we know who are the true kin of Jesus (Lk 8:21).

This society of men and of women, small in number and in status, but great by reason of the revelations it had received and the strength in which it would be clothed, was the nucleus of the first Church. We see it assembled on a terrace of Jerusalem, where the Lord had just visited it. Perhaps they had sensed that this visit might well be the last. The word to Magdalene had not been forgotten: "I ascend to my Father and your Father, my God and your God; do not hold me back." Nor others of the same nature: "It will be better for me as for you that I go away; if you loved me, you would rejoice at the fact that I return to my Father." In any event, he enjoined them that this time they were not to depart from Jerusalem, as opposed to what he had told them to do forty days earlier. At the dawn of the Resurrection, he had ordered them not to tarry in the City; it was in Galilee that he desired to see them again in more relaxed circumstances. Now he said to them: Do not go out of the City again, it is there that you are going to receive the Holy Spirit.

In both of his accounts, Luke refers to this Sending of the Holy Spirit as "the Promise of the Father." This did not mean just any kind of promise, but that which crowned everything, made out of the purest generosity and without having had to be solicited (Lk 24:49; Ac 1:4). Wait for the fulfillment of it in Jerusalem, this will be in a few days, Jesus says. To prepare them for this accomplishment, he recalled to their memories the prophetic declaration which John the Baptist had emphatically repeated (Mk 1:8; Mt 3:11; Lk 3:16; Jn 1:33), at the time of the inaugural baptism which several among them had received and even administered (Jn 1:37, 40, 3:25, 4:1-2): he had them understand that they were going to be "immersed in the Holy Spirit." We have here both the announcement of the extraordinary effusion by which they will be favored within a few days, and of the baptismal immersions which will be the normal continuation of this. For the disciples there was between the ancient order represented by John, and the new order, which began with them, a contrast forcefully marked by these words "But you," in which the conjunction of opposition is joined to a "you" which is full of grandeur.

It was in Jerusalem that there would come about the Coming of the Spirit, which had already been envisioned by the Prophets; and this would be the point of departure for the mission which would be its sequel and first effect (Ac 1:5, 8). The book of the Acts informs us that the disciples conformed to the injunction of the Lord. On Pentecost, sensing that the Promise had been fulfilled, they had no hesitation about what should follow. This is why they remained attached to the Holy City and gave so much importance to the Church at Jerusalem.

They were nonetheless strangers in this town, out of their element in the city, mistreated by the authorities; nothing prevented them from obstinately remaining there or returning there, for ten or twelve years and perhaps more, so that they only withdrew from it little by little, impelled by the Spirit and by events. This conduct reflected the recommendations of Jesus and the concern about being faithful to them. The new Reign had to be offered to all of Judea before being carried even to the ends of the earth.

The Final Rendezvous

When, therefore, he had brought back the various members of his little Church to Jerusalem, Jesus once more closely united himself to them (Ac 1:4), and did for all of them something similar to what he had done for Peter at the sea of Tiberias. "He led them out," Luke writes in his first account (Lk 24:50), and "they went out together," he resumes in his second account (Ac 1:6). This aspect appears to be worth remarking. The texts do not say that the Lord had walked visibly at their head from the interior of the town all the way to one of the high points of the Mount of Olives. Nor do they say at what hour of day or night the last act of the Ascension took place. On this point, tradition does not supply for the silence of the texts. Furthermore, Jesus could have circulated through the streets of the town or along the paths of the outskirts at the head of his disciples without being seen or recognized by others than themselves. Experience had shown that he revealed himself as he wished, in the measure and according to the manner that he wished; his physical condition was completely subordinated to the instigations of his soul. The Lord also could simply have made himself visible at the moment of departure and at the instant of arrival, in order to put his disciples on the road, and then to rejoin them at the top of the Mount.

A new talk is entered upon when they come together at the indicated place. There were several disciples there who multiplied their questions, probably because they knew or they sensed that their Master was going to escape them. One of these questions is reported by Luke. It is not worthy of the situation, which is an appreciable mark of authenticity: no one would have invented it in order to insert it at this moment. Yet it does not have the purely earthbound meaning which would lead one to believe that some of the disciples present were not yet sufficiently penetrated by the teachings of their Master to be lifted above the conceptions of their compatriots.

The question posed by these disciples does not mean that they dreamed of a merely temporal and political kingdom. They asked Jesus if it was in the interest of Israel that he was going to restore the Kingdom. Or, more exactly perhaps, they asked if in the restorations which they saw him making there was a place for their nation and if, in spite of its faults, Israel might still hope for a privileged role. These worthy disciples were quite aware that they were living in days of exceptional significance and that decisive things were happening "during this time," as they said. It could not escape them at the term of the forty days that the Resurrection of Jesus had already inaugurated the Kingdom in an eminently spiritual sense and that events of great moment were being prepared in the same sense. They themselves, imbued with divine revelations, invested with spiritual powers, will have to continue the work and to propagate it throughout the entire world in the sense in which it was instituted. It was most natural that they be eager to know what lot would fall to Israel in a restoration of this quality.

Had not Amos prophesied that "the Lord Yahveh would raise up again the house of David"? (Am 9:11). Had not the first Isaiah announced that Israel would arbitrate among nations and be the judge of numerous peoples? (Is 2:4). And did not the later Isaiah go so far as to predict things like these to his people: "You will spread out in every direction, and your posterity will take possession of the nations and will people deserted towns ... for your Spouse is your Creator, Yahveh of the hosts is his name, and your Redeemer is the Holy One of Israel, he is called the God of all the earth" (Is 54:3-5). Other pronouncements, in the Prophets or in the Psalms, ring with the same sound.

Those of the disciples who knew their Bible the best, those like Philip, Thomas, Bartholomew, Matthew, those whom I have called the intellectuals of the College, might have asked themselves what was going to become of all this, and in what way these prophecies ought to be understood. The disciples whom Luke puts on the scene here make us think of the holy people whom he presented in the Infancy gospel, of Zechariah, of Simeon, completely convinced that the salvation of the world would be brought about through Israel. Furthermore, it would be thus, but in a much more deeply spiritual sense than they could ever have imagined. Nevertheless, their preoccupation was legitimate, it was in no way common. It denoted, on the contrary, a veritable nobility of soul, a learned acquaintance with the Scriptures, a faithfulness, an attentiveness to the promises of the Father.

Jesus answered in tones which qualified the request: he did not say that Israel would not have its hour and its role, but he made it understood that there was a mystery here, one of those the secret of which was reserved to the Father. It does not pertain to you, he explained, to know the times nor the moments. He meant the epoch of fulfillment, and the turn that it would take. He holds back in this regard, as he had for the end of time. It could be that the two events are not unrelated; they are the secret of the Father (Mk 13:32).

In compensation, what is clear, Jesus said to his disciples, is the part that you are to play and the role that is entrusted to you, in the new Kingdom. We read here that they are invested with the great mission, as we have read at the end of Luke's gospel (Lk 24:47-49), in the conclusion of Mark (Mk 16:15), and at the termination of Matthew's gospel (Mt 28:18-20). The command does not have more amplitude here than in the other passages; only, it is very closely connected to the coming of the Holy Spirit. When the Holy Spirit has erupted in you, Jesus says, you will feel sufficient strength within you to be my witnesses, to be men who are fully mine and who are perfectly capable of speaking for me.

There is a statement recorded at this precise spot, one which was not mentioned in the other passages, containing the order according to which the mission ought to develop, and following which it will in fact have its development. We cannot see here merely a geographical description; we should recognize rather the ideal program of the expansion of Christianity. Jerusalem had been the Holy City, the Abode of the Great King: it was from it that the new Law was to come forth (Is 2:3). Next, Judea was to be evangelized, all of Judea, Jesus insisted; and thereby he meant not only the hills of Judah, but Galilee, Perea, all of the regions inhabited by the Jews. Afterwards, you will undertake the remainder of the world, even Samaria, he declared with special intent: to the Samaritan, the neighbor who loves you not and for whom you have no love, an enemy of your race and schismatic from your religion, you are going to offer the new grace, it is for him as well as for the Israelite. And, when you have thus begun to transcend your national and religious frontiers, then you will no longer recognize any sort of border, and you will be my witnesses even to the extremities of the earth. His program was of the dimensions of the globe itself.

To this Luke has conjoined the tableau of the flight by which Jesus desired to signify that he was going to leave this globe. It was the sacrament of the Ascension, the visible sign of the mystery. There is no theophany of the Old Testament which is comparable to this one. The Transfiguration had been but a kind of preparation for it. Jesus offers to his own a view of his departure as a spectacle [this is the literal expression of the text (Ac 1:11)], a spectacle which they would never forget: You will see me ascending to where I first was, he had said to them (Jn 6:62). The manifestation is portrayed in both of the tableaux sketched by Luke (Gospel and Acts): in order to grasp all of its beauty, they must be brought together to complete one another, as it appears that the author wished to be done.

At several of his apparitions, Jesus had effaced himself almost as soon as he had shown himself; this time it is different. After he had spoken to the disciples and perhaps had joined to his declarations a gesture adapted also to the dimensions of the world, he made another gesture, that of raising his hands to heaven and stretching them forth over them as if in order to bless them. This must have been his customary benediction; on this day it had a more marked significance, in liaison with the words which were proclaimed and with the sacred ordination which had just taken place. But what was totally unique was what happened next: in the very gesture of blessing, behold, Jesus was separated from his own and borne away to heaven (Lk 24:51). Prostrate as they were in their adoration (Lk 24:52), they had the clear intuition that their good Master "was going away."

The text of the Acts shows the Lord fading into the distance and the heights slowly and mightily; one could believe that he continued to gaze at them and to bless them. They themselves, from below, had their eyes fixed on him; veritably, they "saw him depart," and this lasted throughout a moment, until the instant when a cloud entered upon the scene, as the text tells us, to carry him still higher and to close him off from their eyes. The cloud, as so many times in the Old Testament, is the sign of God, the symbol of his mystery, the vehicle of his Glory and of his Majesty. A cloud had thus appeared at the Transfiguration (Lk 9:34-35 and parallels). In the most humiliating moments of his Passion, Jesus had told the Jews that he would have in his service the clouds of heaven (Mk 14:62-64; Mt 26:64-65). In the sight of the disciples, the Ascension of Jesus was brought to achievement in the divine cloud (Ac 1:9).

Even after the Lord had disappeared, they continued to stare fixedly in the direction in which they had seen him depart. There is no opposition between the profound prostration to the earth, of the first account (Lk 24:52), and their gaze obstinately turned towards the sky, in the second account (Ac 1:10). At the sight of this ascent, throughout the time that it lasted, the friends and the kin of Jesus, men and women of the most diverse temperaments, must have moved about a great deal. They were not fixed by a set liturgy. All lent fervent attention, with collective enthusiasm but also with individual reactions: some could have prostrated themselves before the divine glory of the event; others remained erect in their attachment to the Lord whom they loved so much; many must have done both as the spectacle evolved and as their feelings diversified. As prepared as they might have been for this departure, the witnesses of the Christ could not have had in advance an exact idea of what it would be like nor have foreseen the actual scene. Visions of this nature are beyond ordinary experience; those who see them can afterwards recall them most vividly, but would not be able to represent them for themselves prior to their happening.

We also might very well think that the Ascension, as it unfolded before the eyes of the disciples, was accompanied by a revelation to their minds; each of them received this revelation of the mystery according to his supernatural capacity. Those who were great received it on a great scale. Peter, John, Thomas, Nathanael, and others, felt themselves enlightened to the most profound depths of their heart; the formulae of faith shone with brilliant splendor within their understanding. "He gloriously ascended to Heaven, and he took his seat at the right of God." Among the women, several also entered profoundly into the mystery. More than any, Mary the mother of Jesus; in the last act just as in the first of the career of her Son, she was there observing and retaining everything in order to meditate upon it in her heart (Ac 1:14; Lk 2:19, 51).

The Mystery of Jesus

The disciples had so fastened their gaze upon the sky, that they did not even notice the two angels who had just posted themselves beside them. The two messengers were only perceived when they began to speak. The author of the Acts does not write "two angels" but, as in the gospel (Lk 24:4), "two men," personages of note, clothed in the adornment of the white robe. It is quite clear that in the thought of the narrator these were two angels, who once more make themselves visible in the role of servants and of heralds of the Lord Jesus.

In the gospel of Luke, there are angels at all the great moments of the life of Jesus; they announce his coming, sing the praises of his nativity, attract visitors to his crib (Lk 1-2). However, Luke does not mention the presence of the good angels at the emergence from the temptation (Lk 4:13) while Mark and Matthew do so (Mk 1:13; Mt 4:11); only, in compensation, he recounts the assistance of the angel at the agony (Lk 22:43). According to the four evangelists, the angels were the overseers of the empty tomb and the first to announce the Resurrection (Mk 16:5; Mt 28:3; Lk 24:4; Jn 20:12). It is not surprising that we find them again at the Ascension.

With a great deal of respect they hail the disciples, particularly the chief ones, with the title of Galileans. In the present case this designation is significant. It is the indication that these men, at least the Eleven, were in majority, if not in totality, Galileans. Perhaps it also reminded them that it was with this quality that they had been chosen, and that in spite of their belonging to Galilee they would have to act mightily in Jerusalem and in Judea. Their strength was in him who had just left them, and who would not cease to assist them. The disciples were brought back to the thought of their mission.

At the same time, they were invited never to forget the departure of Jesus. The angels did not say, notice carefully: As you have seen him going away, you will see him come back. There is not the least trace, in their message, of a proximate return of the Lord. The angels say: He will come back as he had departed, in his same human substance, with his same glorious body, and also in the same majestic array; the spectacle which he has created at his departure, he will create at the moment of his great return. The word of the text designating "this spectacle" is employed for things which arouse astonishment and provoke a keen wonder. But the angels in no way say when, or before whose eyes, the spectacle of the return will take place.

It has been asked, nevertheless, whether they did not mean that it would take place at the same point of our sphere where the departure had been effected: this question is quite secondary. The principal thing is to realize that the Lord Christ, the Master of the new heaven and the new earth (Rv 21:1; 2 P 3:13), is constituted there as the center of every corporal resurrection. When the moment which is marked down among the divine secrets has come, he will make his glorious breakthrough: he will shine like lightning from one end of the world to the other (Lk 17:24); he will come upon every creature and particularly upon every spirit with great power and great glory (Lk 21:27). Everything that will have been saved through him will rush body and soul towards him as forcefully as vultures towards their prey (Lk 17:37). He will gather his elect from the four winds of humanity, and with them he will people a great space, from the extremity of earth to the extremity of heaven (Mk 13:27; Mt 24:31).

Luke tells us, at the end of the first account, that the disciples went back to Jerusalem filled with a great joy (Lk 24:52). It was this that Jesus had recommended to them when he had said: "If you loved me, you would rejoice at the fact that I am going to the Father" (Jn 14:28), or again: "When I have seen you again, you will feel deep within yourselves a joy such that no one will be capable of taking it from you" (Jn 16:22).

Luke informs us finally, and this is in fact the last word of his gospel, that these Galilean friends of Jesus did dwell in Jerusalem as he had instructed them, and were constantly in the Temple or, as good Israelites faithful to their holy places, they were ceaselessly blessing God (Lk 24:53). This thanksgiving of the disciples after the Lord's Ascension is extremely moving. They give thanks to God, the Father of Our Lord Jesus Christ (Col 1:3). Full of joy, they express their gratitude to the Father who had made them capable of participating in the heritage of the saints in the light, and who had snatched them from the power of darkness to transport them into the Kingdom of his beloved Son, in whose communion true redemption, the forgiveness of sins, was assured them (Col 1:11-14).

Their faith in the mystery of Jesus revolved about the thoughts cited above, which constituted the theme of the first addresses of Peter to the people and to the authorities. Death had not been able to retain any hold whatsoever on him whom he calls by the decorous name of "the Archegos, the Incomparable Conductor of Life" (Ac 3:15), he who commands but also he who begins, the Prince, the Principle. For the disciples, witnesses of facts which were beyond them, the essential thing was to believe that Jesus had entered into the existence of his veritable greatness.

They recalled that he had said to the Jews: "You will die in your sins, if you do not believe that I Am" (Jn 8:24), and to themselves: "You must believe that I Am" (Jn 13:19). Long before his death, he had affirmed his proper existence in this surprising fashion which was in a way absolute; the terms which he used singularly resembled those by which the most inspired prophets had expressed the existence of the Lord Yahveh (Is 41:4, 43:10, 25, 52:6); the words of Jesus flamed like those of the burning Bush (Ex 3:14).

Even at the depths of his abasement, and, if we dare speak thus, at the lowest point of his Incarnation (Ph 2:8), when he was the most entangled with mortals and exposed himself the most to death, he did not cease to assert a sovereign existence: "Before Abraham existed, I Am" (Jn 8:58) he cried out one day. And, when he saw death coming, it was nothing else for him than a fuller development of his whole being, the gate of entry into his transcendent survival: "And now, Father, glorify me at your side with the same glory which was mine with you before the world came into existence" (Jn 17:5). Then, not willing to return alone into this glory, he pursues his prayer and amplifies its force: "Father," he said, "I will that where I am, these also (whom you have given me) be with me, so that they may see my glory, for you have loved me before the creation of the world" (Jn 17:24).

It was upon elements of this kind, received from the very mouth of their Master, that was exercised the thought of the first disciples. As the angels had them understand, the Ascension in taking Jesus from them helped them to contemplate him in the full grandeur of his mystery; it helped them to situate him as true Man and true God in his Unique Personality of Son of God. Concerning the Person and the Work of the Christ, Paul, the rabbi of old, the neo-convert, will tranquilly write the following:

> This Son is the image of the invisible God, the first born of all creation. In effect, it was in him that everything has been created, in heaven and on earth, the visible world and the invisible world, the Thrones, the Lordships, the Principalities, the Powers. Indeed, everything has been created by him and for him. Yes, he exists before all things, and everything subsists in him. It is he who is also at the head of his Body, that is, the Church. He is the beginning, the first born from among the dead. He must, then, in all things, be the First. For it has pleased God to cause to reside in him the entire pleroma [plenitude of existence, or plenitude of divine gifts]. It has pleased God to make use of him to bring about his reconciliation with all things: after he had reestablished peace through the blood which this Christ had shed upon the cross, through him he was able to extend this peace, to what is on earth, and to what is in heaven (Col 1:15-20).